CHRISTMAS CAKE BOOK

ELAINE MACGREGOR

MEREHURST

I would like to thank my husband, Stuart MacGregor, who has put all my half-formed words into English

Published in 1993 by Merehurst Limited, Ferry House,
51–57 Lacy Road, Putney, London SW15 1PR

Reprinted 1993, 1995
Paperback edition published 1994

ISBN 1-85391-269-7 (hardback)
ISBN 1-85391-423-1 (paperback)

 A catalogue record for this book is available from the British Library.

Edited by Bridget Jones
Designed by Jo Tapper
Photography by Zul Mukhida
Colour Separation by Scantrans, Singapore
Printed by Canale, Italy

NOTES ON USING THE RECIPES

For all recipes, quantities are given in metric, Imperial and cup measurements. Follow one set of measures only as they are not interchangeable. Standard 5ml teaspoons (tsp) and 15ml tablespoons (tbsp) are used. Australian readers, whose tablespoons measure 20ml, should adjust quantities accordingly. All spoon measures are assumed to be level unless otherwise stated.

Eggs are a standard size 3 (medium) unless otherwise stated.

CONTENTS

BASIC RECIPES

SWISS (JELLY) ROLL

3 large eggs
90g (3 oz/⅓ cup) caster (superfine) sugar
90g (3 oz/¼ cup) plain (all-purpose) flour, sifted and left in a warm place

EQUIPMENT

30 x 20cm (12 x 8 inch) Swiss roll tin (jelly roll pan)
non-stick baking spray, non-stick paper or teflon-coated baking sheet
clean tea-towel

Preheat the oven to 230°C (450°F/Gas 8). Spray the tin (pan) with non-stick baking spray or grease and line it with non-stick paper or teflon-coated baking sheet.

Put the eggs and sugar into the large mixing bowl and place this over a saucepan of hot water on low heat. Whisk the mixture by hand, preferably using a balloon whisk, until it thickens and becomes light and fluffy. The whisk should leave a trail over the surface as it is lifted. It takes about 10 minutes of whisking to achieve this consistency. Do not stop or the mixture will settle.

Remove the bowl from the saucepan and gently fold in the flour. The mixture should resemble lightly whipped cream: if it is too thick, fold in a few drops of warm water. Pour the mixture into the prepared tin and spread it evenly. Bake for 8 – 10 minutes, until risen, golden and springy to the touch.

Meanwhile, lay a sheet of non-stick paper on a dampened tea-towel and sprinkle with caster (superfine) sugar. Cut another sheet of non-stick paper just bigger than the tin. As soon as the cake is cooked, turn it out onto the sugared paper.

Trim all the edges and make a shallow cut across the cake about 2.5cm (1 inch) from one narrow edge. This will allow the cake to roll more easily. The cake may be spread with jam (conserve) and must then be rolled immediately. Alternatively, lay the second sheet of paper on top of the cake and roll it up inside the cake. Use the tea-towel and sugared paper as a guide for lifting and rolling the cake, see page 27. When cool, the cake can be unrolled, the paper removed and a filling added.

Makes a 20cm(8 inch) long Swiss (jelly) roll

SPONGE CAKE

250g (8 oz/1 cup) butter or margarine
250g (8 oz/1¼ cups) caster (superfine) sugar
4 eggs, lightly beaten
250g (8 oz/2 cups) self-raising flour, sifted

EQUIPMENT

20cm (8 inch) round cake tin (pan)
non-stick baking spray, non-stick paper or teflon-coated baking sheet

Preheat the oven to 190°C (375°F/Gas 5). Grease and flour the tin (pan). Make sure the excess flour is knocked out of the tin. Alternatively, spray the tin with non-stick baking spray or line it with teflon-coated baking sheet.

Cream the butter or margarine and sugar together until light and fluffy. Gradually add the eggs and mix well, adding a spoonful of the flour. Fold in the flour (do not beat it in) and turn the mixture into the prepared tin.

Bake for about 45 minutes or until a skewer inserted into the centre of the cake comes out clean. When fully cooked the cake should spring back when lightly touched and it should have slightly shrunk away from the sides of the tin. Leave the cake to cool in the tin for 2 – 3 minutes, then turn it out onto a wire rack or sugared paper.

Makes a 20cm (8 inch) round cake

MADEIRA CAKE

185g (6 oz/¾ cup) unsalted butter
185g (6 oz/¾ cup) caster (superfine) sugar
4 large eggs
185g (6 oz/1½ cups) self-raising flour
90 (3 oz/¾ cup) plain (all-purpose) flour
1 teaspoon lemon juice

EQUIPMENT

20cm (8 inch) round cake tin (pan)
non-stick baking spray, non-stick paper or teflon-coated baking sheet

PERFECT CAKE MIXTURES

When making creamed mixtures, gradually mix in the eggs, adding a little of the measured flour as this prevents curdling. It is not a disaster if the mixture does curdle but the result will not be as light and even.

Preheat the oven to 160°C (325°F/Gas 3). Spray the tin (pan) with non-stick baking spray or grease and line it with non-stick paper or teflon-coated baking sheet.

Cream the butter and sugar until light and fluffy. Gradually mix in the eggs, adding a spoonful of the flour. Sift the flours together thoroughly and fold them into the mixture. Fold in the lemon juice and turn the mixture into the prepared tin.

Bake for about 1 hour 10 minutes, or until a skewer inserted in the centre of the cake comes out clean. Leave the cake to cool in the tin for 2 – 3 minutes, then turn it out onto a wire rack or sugared paper.

Makes a 20cm (8 inch) round cake

QUICK MADEIRA CAKE

500g (1 lb/4 cups) plain (all-purpose) flour
2 teaspoons baking powder
440g (14 oz/2 cups) caster (superfine) sugar
440g (14 oz/2 cups) soft margarine
7 eggs
3½ tablespoons milk
EQUIPMENT
20cm (8 inch) square or 23cm (9 inch) round cake tin (pan)
non-stick baking spray, non-stick paper or teflon-coated baking sheet

Preheat the oven to 160°C (325°F/Gas 3). Spray the tin (pan) with non-stick baking spray or grease and line it with non-stick paper or teflon-coated baking sheet. Sift the flour and baking powder into a bowl. Add the sugar, margarine, eggs and milk, and mix together. Beat for 1 minute if using an electric mixer or for 2 – 3 minutes by hand.

Turn the mixture into the prepared tin and bake for 1¾ – 2 hours, or until a skewer inserted into the centre of the cake comes out clean.

Makes a 20cm (8 inch) square or 23cm (9 inch) round cake

Sponge cakes are light and quick to make. Three classic recipes are shown here.
Top to bottom: *Sponge Cake, Swiss (Jelly) Roll and Madeira Cake*

ADAPTING CAKE RECIPE QUANTITIES TO DIFFERENT BAKING TINS (PANS)

When converting from a round to a square tin (pan), use one which is 2.5cm (1 inch) smaller. For example, the Quick Madeira Cake may be baked in a 23cm (9 inch) round tin or a square tin which is 2.5cm (1 inch) smaller: 20cm (8 inch). To decide on the amount of mixture for a tin of unusual shape, fill the tin with water, then measure the volume of water. Compare this to the volume of water needed to fill the tin. suggested in the recipe. If the suggested tin is smaller; then reduce the recipe quantities proportionally; if it is larger, then increase them by the correct proportions.

GINGERBREAD

500g (1 lb/4 cups) plain (all-purpose) flour
1 rounded teaspoon bicarbonate of soda (baking soda)
2 teaspoons ground ginger
185g (6 oz/¾ cup) butter or margarine
315g (10 oz/2 cups) dark soft brown sugar
186g (6 oz/½ cup) golden syrup (light corn syrup)
2 eggs, lightly beaten
EQUIPMENT
baking sheets
non-stick baking spray, non-stick paper or
teflon-coated baking sheet

Preheat the oven to 190°C (375°F/Gas 5). Spray the baking sheets with non-stick baking spray or grease and line them with non-stick paper or teflon-coated baking sheet. Sift the flour, bicarbonate of soda and ground ginger together. Rub in the butter or margarine until the mixture resembles fine breadcrumbs, then add the sugar and mix well.

Warm the syrup sufficiently to make it flow easily and stir it into the rubbed-in mixture with the egg to make a pliable dough. Knead the dough until smooth, then roll it out thinly on a floured worksurface. Cut out the required shapes and place them carefully on the baking sheets. Bake for 8 – 10 minutes, until evenly browned.

Makes 1.25kg (2½ lb), about 40.5 x 30cm (17 x 12 inch) rolled out

BOILED FRUIT CAKE

250g (8 oz/2 cups) butter or margarine
185g (6 oz/1 cup) soft brown sugar
4 tablespoons black treacle or molasses
4 teaspoons ground mixed spice (apple-pie spice)
1 teaspoon almond essence (extract)
1 teaspoon vanilla essence (extract)
1.5kg (3 lb/9 cups) mixed dried fruit
4 tablespoons brandy, sherry or orange juice
4 eggs
315 g (10 oz/2½ cups) plain (all-purpose) or
self-raising (self-rising) flour
EQUIPMENT
23cm (9 inch) round cake tin (pan)
non-stick paper or brown paper

Mix the butter or margarine, sugar, treacle or molasses, ground mixed spice, almond and vanilla essences, dried fruit and brandy, sherry or orange juice in a large saucepan and heat gently for 5 minutes until the sugar has dissolved and the ingredients are well combined. Allow the mixture to cool, then add the eggs and stir in the flour.

Turn the mixture into the prepared tin (pan) and bake for 4 hours, until a skewer inserted into the centre of the cake comes out clean. Leave the cake to cool before turning it out of the tin.

Makes a 23cm (9 inch) round cake

LIGHT FRUIT CAKE

250g (8 oz/1½ cups) mixed dried fruit
60ml (2 fl oz/¼ cup) sherry or orange juice
250g (8 oz/1 cup) butter or margarine
250g (8 oz/1¼ cups) caster (superfine) sugar
4 eggs, lightly beaten
250g (8 oz/2 cups) plain (all-purpose) flour
EQUIPMENT
20cm (8 inch) round cake tin (pan)
non-stick paper or brown paper

Soak the mixed dried fruit in the sherry or orange juice overnight to plump out the fruit. Preheat the oven to 160°C (325°F/Gas 3). Line the tin (pan) with non-stick or brown paper.

Cream the butter and sugar until light and fluffy. Gradually add the eggs. Stir in the soaked fruit, then gently fold in the flour. Turn the mixture into the tin, smooth the top, making a slight dip in the centre and bake for 1½ hours. Leave the cake to cool before turning it out of the tin.

Makes a 20cm (8 inch) round cake

HANDY HINT

The versatile boiled fruit cake recipe can be made with either plain (all-purpose) or self-raising (self-rising) flour because of the large quantity of fruit which prevents the mixture from rising and peaking excessively or sinking in the middle.

RICH FRUIT CAKE

250g (8 oz/1½ cups) sultanas (golden raisins)
250g (8 oz/1⅓ cups) currants
250g (8 oz/1½ cups) raisins
125g (4 oz/⅔ cup) glacé (candied) cherries, halved
60g (2 oz/⅓ cup) blanched almonds, chopped
125ml (4 fl oz/½ cup) brandy, sherry or orange juice
250g (8 oz/2 cups) plain (all-purpose) flour
60g (2 oz/½ cup) self-raising (self-rising) flour
1 teaspoon each of ground mixed spice (apple-pie spice) and ground cinnamon
¼ teaspoon grated nutmeg
pinch of salt
60g (2 oz/½ cup) ground almonds
250g (8 oz/1 cup) butter
250g (8 oz/1½ cups) dark soft brown sugar
4 eggs, lightly beaten
EQUIPMENT
20cm (8 inch) round cake tin (pan)
non-stick paper or brown paper

Soak the dried fruit, cherries and chopped almonds overnight in the brandy, sherry or orange juice.

Preheat the oven 140°C (275°F/Gas 1). Line the tin (pan) with non-stick or brown paper. Sift both flours, the spices and ground almonds together. Cream the butter and sugar together until light and soft, then gradually add the eggs. Stir in the flour and fruit, adding a little at a time of first one, then the other. Do not beat.

Turn the mixture into the prepared tin and bake for 3½ – 4 hours, until a skewer inserted into the centre of the cake comes out clean. Leave the cake to cool in the tin.

Fruit cakes are usually favoured for important celebrations and the alternative varieties are illustrated here.
Top to bottom: *Boiled Fruit Cake, Light Fruit Cake and traditional Rich Fruit Cake.*

NUTS FOR RICH FRUIT CAKE

Other nuts, such as walnuts, hazelnuts, pecans or brazils, may be used instead of blanched almonds in the Rich Fruit Cake recipe.

COATINGS AND ICINGS

Marzipan or Almond Paste

Commercial marzipan is made by grinding blanched almonds, adding the resulting paste to sugar and roasting the mixture. Marzipan is an expensive product but almond paste, which contains a lower proportion of almonds, is good and it is cheaper than top-quality marzipan. Cheapest of all are marzipan substitutes made with apricot kernels and almond flavouring.

Storing Marzipan

Marzipan should be well wrapped in an airtight polythene bag and stored in the refrigerator. If it dries, it can be moistened with a little boiled water, liquid glucose (clear corn syrup) or glycerine (glycerol).

MARZIPAN

This quick-drying marzipan or almond paste is not oily and it will remain pliable for 3 – 4 weeks with correct storage. It is best to make the almond paste the day before it is required.

500g (1 lb/2 cups) sugar
155ml (5 fl oz/⅔ cup) plus 4 tablespoons water
large pinch of cream of tartar
375g (12 oz/3½ cups) ground almonds
2 egg whites
about 450g (1 lb/3 cups) icing (confectioners') sugar, sifted
almond essence (extract), optional

EQUIPMENT

sugar thermometer
marble slab or heavy-duty chopping board
metal spatula

Warm the sugar and water in a large saucepan over very gentle heat. Stir with a metal spoon to dissolve the sugar. Do not boil until every grain of sugar has dissolved. Add the cream of tartar, then bring the syrup to the boil. Boil rapidly, without stirring, until the syrup reaches 118°C (245°F), the soft ball stage.

Do not overboil as this will make the almond paste difficult to handle. To test the syrup, drop a teaspoonful of it into a cup of cold water – it should form a soft ball when removed and rubbed between the fingers. Stop the syrup cooking by placing the base of the saucepan in cold water, then immediately stir in the ground almonds and egg whites. Return the pan to low heat and stir until the mixture thickens slightly.

Turn the paste out onto a marble slab or heavy-duty chopping board and work it with a metal spatula, scraping it from the edges to the middle in a folding motion, until it cools and thickens. When the paste is cool, knead it by hand until it is smooth, working in the icing (confectioners') sugar. It will take up to half its weight in icing sugar. For extra flavour, add a few drops of almond essence. Store the paste in an airtight jar or a thick polythene bag until ready to use.

Makes 1kg (2lb)

BOILED SUGARPASTE

This recipe makes an elastic sugarpaste that is easy to handle: make it at least a day prior to use.

30g (1 oz/2 tablespoons) powdered gelatine
315ml (10 fl oz/1¼ cups) water
500g (1 lb/2 cups) sugar
125g (4 oz/⅓ cup) liquid glucose (clear corn syrup)
1 tablespoon glycerine (glycerol)
1 teaspoon cream of tartar
125g (4 oz/½ cup) white vegetable fat (shortening)
1.5kg (3 lb/9 cups) icing (confectioners') sugar, sifted

EQUIPMENT

sugar thermometer
metal spatula

Sprinkle the gelatine over half the water in a small heatproof bowl. Leave to soften for 2 – 3 minutes, until spongy. Stand the bowl over a saucepan of hot (not boiling) water and stir the gelatine until it has dissolved completely.

Meanwhile, place the sugar, glucose (clear corn syrup), glycerine (glycerol), cream of tartar and the remaining water in a wide, heavy-based saucepan over medium heat and stir until every grain of sugar has dissolved. Bring to the boil, making sure no sugar crystals adhere to the side of the saucepan. Boil over high heat until the temperature reaches 118°C (245°F), the soft ball stage.

Remove the pan from the heat immediately and place it in a bowl of cold water to stop the cooking process. Cool for 3 – 4 minutes, then stir in the fat (shortening) and the dissolved gelatine.

Mix in the icing (confectioners') sugar a cupful at a time to make a soft paste, then knead in the remaining sugar until smooth and pliable. Leave in an airtight container for 24 hours before use. If necessary, knead in extra icing sugar to obtain a dry, non-sticky consistency.

Makes about 2.5kg (5 lb)

UNCOOKED SUGARPASTE

This recipe is simple to make; however, it does not have the fine texture or elasticity of boiled sugarpaste.

2 teaspoons liquid glucose (clear corn syrup)
1 egg white
1kg (2 lb/6 cups) icing (confectioners') sugar
½ teaspoon glycerine (glycerol)
juice of ½ lemon

Warm the glucose over hot water to make it runny. Beat the egg white and add 375g (12 oz/2¼ cups) of the icing (confectioners') sugar. Beat well until the mixture begins to stiffen. Add the lemon juice and beat again. Mix in another 250g (8 oz/1½ cups) of the sugar and beat thoroughly. Add the glycerine (glycerol) and glucose (clear corn syrup) and continue beating in more icing sugar until the mixture thickens.

Once the paste is stiff, turn it out onto a worksurface dusted with icing (confectioners') sugar and knead it until it loses all signs of stickiness. The paste can be used immediately but is best placed in an airtight container and left overnight.

Makes about 1kg (2 lb)

AMERICAN BUTTERCREAM

This freezes well. It may also be made with half butter and half white vegetable fat (shortening).

125g (4 oz/½ cup) white vegetable fat (shortening)
1 teaspoon vanilla or butter essence (extract)
pinch of salt
500g (1 lb/3 cups) icing (confectioners') sugar
3 tablespoons milk

Beat the fat until it is soft, then add the vanilla or butter essence and salt. Beat in the icing (confectioners') sugar a little at a time, scraping down the sides of the bowl regularly. Add the milk and beat at high speed, until the buttercream is light and fluffy. Keep well covered in the refrigerator when not in use.

Makes about 625g (1¼ lb/3½ cups)

ROYAL ICING

5 teaspoons pure powdered albumen
90ml (3 fl oz) water
500g (1 lb/3 cups) icing (confectioners') sugar, sifted
1 teaspoon glycerine (glycerol), see method

Stir the albumen into the water and leave for 30 minutes, until it has dissolved completely. Strain the albumen into a bowl and add half the icing (confectioners') sugar. Beat the mixture on the slowest speed if using an electric mixer, or for 100 strokes by hand, until it is smooth. Add the icing to the remaining sugar and continue beating for about 10 minutes on low speed. The icing is the right consistency when it has a satin-like appearance and it stands in soft peaks.

Add the glycerine (glycerol) if the icing is to be used for covering a cake. This prevents the icing from setting too hard. Glycerine is not added to icing which is used for piping or run-outs.

Makes about 500g (1 lb)

ROYAL ICING MADE WITH FRESH EGG WHITE

Royal icing can also be made with fresh egg white. Allow 375g (12 oz/2 cups) icing (confectioners') sugar to 1 egg white. Break up the egg white with a palette knife and add the icing sugar a dessertspoonful at a time. Beat it thoroughly by hand between additions of sugar. A squeeze of lemon juice will help to give the icing a whiter appearance.

GUM ARABIC GLUE

3 teaspoons water
1 teaspoon gum arabic

Measure the water into a small screw-top jar and add the gum arabic. Shake well until the gum arabic has dissolved. Keep the mixture in the refrigerator when not in use.

HANDY HINT

Sugarpaste can be modified to make it set slightly harder by kneading in a little gum tragacanth (1 teaspoon to 500 g/1 lb sugarpaste). It dries more quickly, for example when making frills. To make the paste slightly more elastic, add CMC or Tylose to it, then it can be used for making simple flowers. If you knead ready-mixed pastillage with sugarpaste, in a ratio of about 50:50, it will make a slower drying paste which is ideal for delicate sugar modelling.

ROYAL ICING

Royal icing is a mixture of finely powdered sugar and egg white. It is the traditional covering for celebration cakes and, since it was introduced about two hundred years ago, it has been the most important element in cake decorating.

PASTILLAGE

There are many different recipes for pastillage, which is also called gum paste, mexican paste, flower paste and petal paste. For convenience I use a purchased mix which is made up by adding water. There are some occasions when the paste dries too quickly, so to overcome this I mix the made-up pastillage with sugarpaste. Most pastillage becomes more elastic and easier to use if it is made up the day before it is required.

PASTILLAGE

This is the collective name for many types of strengthened sugarpastes or gum pastes, all of which have similar uses. Use the recipe or paste which you prefer – I always recommend trying them all to find your favourite.

GUM PASTE (1)

250g (8 oz/1½ cups) icing (confectioners') sugar, sifted
3 teaspoons gum tragacanth or CMC
1 teaspoon liquid glucose (clear corn syrup)
5 – 6 teaspoons cold water

Sift the icing (confectioners') sugar and gum tragacanth or CMC together. Make a depression in the middle of the sugar and add the liquid glucose (clear corn syrup). Add the water and mix well. Knead well until smooth and pliable. Wrap tightly in polythene and place in an airtight container, then leave for 24 hours.

GUM PASTE (2)

500g (1 lb/3 cups) icing (confectioners') sugar , sifted
1 large egg white
3 teaspoons gum tragacanth or CMC
2 teaspoons liquid glucose (clear corn syrup)
2 teaspoons powdered gelatine
5 teaspoons cold water
2 teaspoons white vegetable fat (shortening)
EQUIPMENT
electric mixer

Warm the sugar and gum tragacanth or CMC in a large bowl over a saucepan of hot water. Cover the bowl, so that the sugar does not form a crust. Sprinkle the gelatine over the water and set aside for 30 minutes. Melt the liquid glucose (clear corn syrup), fat (shortening) and gelatine over very low heat.

Once the sugar is warm, stir it on slow speed. Add the liquid mixture and the egg white. Turn the machine to maximum speed and beat the paste for about 15 minutes. The longer and harder it is beaten, the whiter the paste will become.

GUM PASTE (3)

75g (2½ oz) egg white
500g (1 lb/3 cups) icing (confectioners') sugar, sifted
3 tablespoons Tylose, gum tragacanth or CMC
1 tablespoon white vegetable fat (shortening)
cornflour (cornstarch), see method

Make up royal icing with the egg white and sugar, see page 9. Then add the Tylose, gum tragacanth or CMC and mix well. The mixture will immediately start to thicken.

Turn the paste out onto a board dusted with icing (confectioners') sugar and knead in the fat (shortening). Wrap the paste well and place in an airtight container, then leave it for at least 24 hours. Knead the paste again. If the paste seems sticky, add a little icing sugar or cornflour (cornstarch).

EDIBLE GUM

Gum tragacanth is an edible plant gum which has been put to various culinary uses for centuries. It has been used for many years to harden gum pastes. CMC stands for carboxymethyl cellulose, a man-made edible gum. Tylose is a brand name for a particular type of CMC. These gums are used to make the paste more elastic and pliable.

THICKNESS GUIDE

Use the diagram shown here to give the correct thickness for sugarpaste and pastillage.

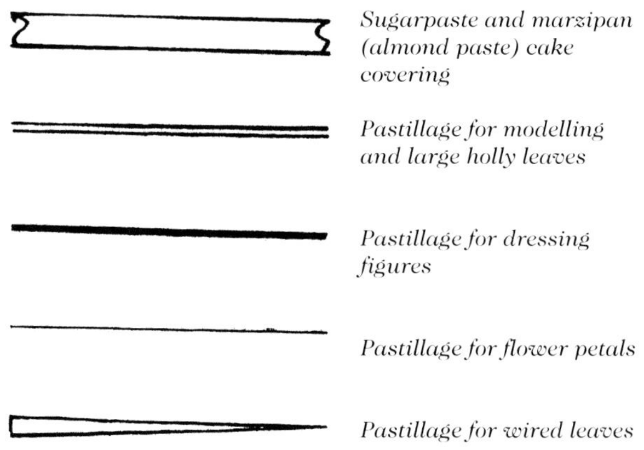

BASIC TECHNIQUES

COATING CAKES WITH MARZIPAN

If the cake is to be covered with sugarpaste, then the marzipan (almond paste) is applied in the same way. Trim the top edge of the cake with a sausage of marzipan, then turn the cake over and brush it with boiled, sieved apricot jam or piping gel. Roll out enough marzipan to cover the top and sides of the cake and follow the instructions given on the right. Allow the marzipan to harden for 24 hours.

If a cake is to be royal iced, the method is as follows and the bottom of the cake is the surface to be iced.

1 Roll out a sausage of marzipan and lay it around the top edge of the cake, sticking it in place with boiled, sieved apricot jam or piping gel. Roll out the marzipan larger than the cake and brush with piping gel. Stand the cake on the paste and trim the bottom edge with a palette knife.

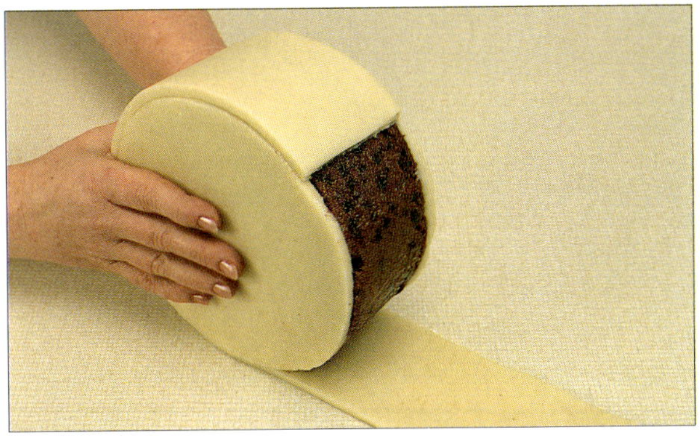

2 Roll out a long, rectangular strip of marzipan measuring three times the diameter of a round cake . Brush the paste with piping gel. Place the cake at one end of the strip, then roll it onto the paste. Press the marzipan gently into place with a smoother, so that the top edge is square and smooth.

COATING CAKES WITH SUGARPASTE

Sugarpaste is flexible and fairly elastic, rather like uncooked pastry, so it follows the contours of a cake very accurately, making it ideal for covering cakes of uneven or irregular shapes. In fact, it is helpful if the edges and corners over which the sugarpaste is laid are not too sharp. For this reason, if a cake is covered with marzipan (almond paste), it is best to drape the marzipan across the entire surface in one piece, rather than covering the top and sides separately.

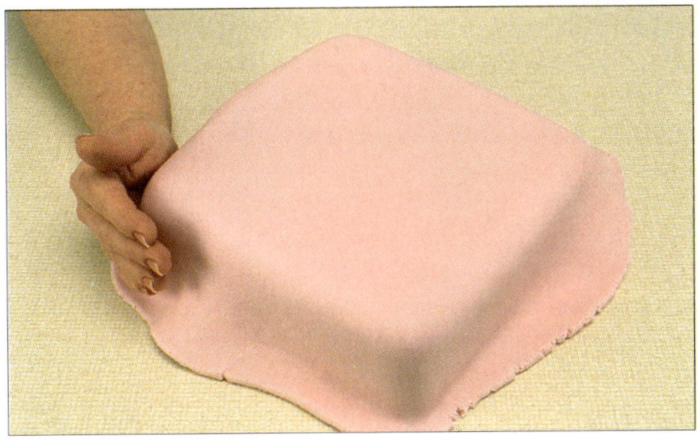

1 Sugarpaste is rolled out and draped over a cake. Always smooth the paste onto the corners first, using the palm of your hand to work it firmly onto the cake. Do not allow the paste to form pleats – if necessary, flare it outwards gently, then squeeze it back against the side of the cake.

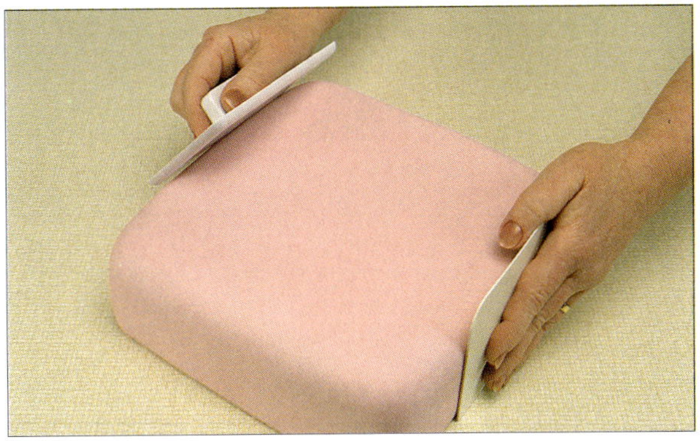

2 Use two smoothers to smooth the paste: hold the cake steady with one while using an ironing action with the other to flatten and smooth the icing. Work on the sides, then the cake top. When the top is satisfactory, finish the sides, paying special attention to the edges and corners.

HANDY HINTS

- *Marzipan or almond paste can be coloured with food colours by kneading the colour into it. It is often used for modelling work and also for making bite-sized sweetmeats and petit-fours.*
- *Place almond paste or marzipan in a warm place to soften it and make it easier to knead.*

MARZIPAN

There are recipes for marzipan to be found in cookery books written over three hundred years ago, when it was used in making macaroons and biscuits, but today it is more commonly used for covering cakes such as battenburg or rich fruit cake

COLOURED SUGARPASTE

Manufacturers make sugarpaste in a variety of colours, so there is no need for you to colour it yourself unless to want to match a particular shade.

COATING CAKES WITH ROYAL ICING

The action of beating together the sugar and egg gives royal icing its biscuit-like texture by incorporating millions of tiny bubbles. Icing which is inadequately beaten will be hard and will crumble and crack when it is cut. Well-made icing can be cut easily with a sharp knife.

It is very important to ensure that the bowl in which you make royal icing is completely free of grease as any contamination prevents the mixture from becoming properly aerated. It is also advisable to beat royal icing in a metal or china bowl rather than plastic which is more difficult to wash completely clean.

If you are concerned about the dangers of salmonella from fresh eggs, the icing can be made from dried, pasteurised powdered egg white or albumen. Simply mix the albumen with water, let it dissolve properly and use it in the same way as fresh egg white. Albumen is also ideal for meringues.

Adding a few drops of lemon juice to royal icing will help to whiten it and also give it a little extra elasticity. This is an advantage when you are using fine piping tubes (tips); but it makes the icing more brittle, so do not add lemon juice to icing used for covering cakes. Allow 1 teaspoon glycerine (glycerol) to each 500 g (1 lb/3 cups) of icing (confectioners') sugar used to make icing for coating a little softer when it has dried on the cake.

A really smooth finish requires at least three separate applications of icing and each layer should dry for a day before the next is applied. Therefore, you must allow plenty of time when coating a cake with royal icing.

1 Apply royal icing across the top of the cake with a palette knife. Spread the icing from side to side in a paddling motion until it is evenly dispersed, rotating the turntable at the same time. Pressing and working the icing with the knife blade helps to burst any air bubbles it contains.

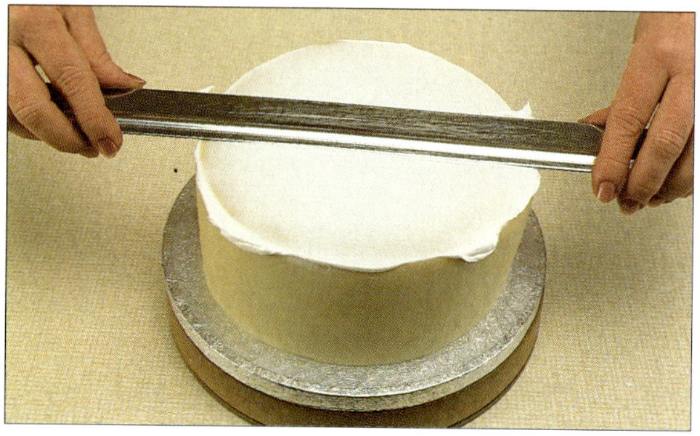

2 Smooth the icing with a metal straight edge. Beginning at the far side of the cake, draw the blade steadily towards you. When you reach the near side, turn the blade over so that its other edge is touching the icing, and push it away from you to the far side of the cake. Do this three or four times. By turning the straight edge over, the icing only builds up on one side.

3 Use a scraper to smooth the icing around the cake sides. Hold it at an angle of about 45 degrees to the cake and rotate the cake through one complete turn of the turntable. The secret of a smooth finish is to rotate the turntable and the cake while holding the scraper steady.

HANDY HINT

Beat icing for piping or coating to eliminate any large air bubbles each time you use it. It should have a silky sheen and be stiff enough to hold itself in swirls and peaks before settling slowly.

COLOURING ROYAL ICING

When colouring icing, always use specialist cake decorating colours which are available in the form of syrups or pastes. They are far stronger than most of the liquid colours to be found in supermarkets. To obtain really strong reds, greens or black, mix the colour with the icing and allow it to stand, covered with a damp cloth, for about 1 hour. During this time the icing will 'wet out' the colour, making it appear stronger and brighter than when first mixed. Powder colours can be dissolved with a few drops of clear alcohol, such as vodka, and then added to the icing.

PIPING TECHNIQUES

It is important to check that the royal icing is of a suitable consistency. Day-old icing is best for most purposes, as the ingredients will have become thoroughly mixed on standing. Always remember to beat the icing by hand in a clean bowl using a palette knife before transferring to a piping bag. The icing should be light and fluffy, and it should hold a firm peak, sinking very slowly back when you test it with the knife blade.

A paper piping bag is far easier to use than an icing syringe. Paper bags should be made of vegetable parchment as this remains waterproof for several hours, so the bags do not split open as easily as those made of greaseproof paper.

MAKING A PIPING BAG

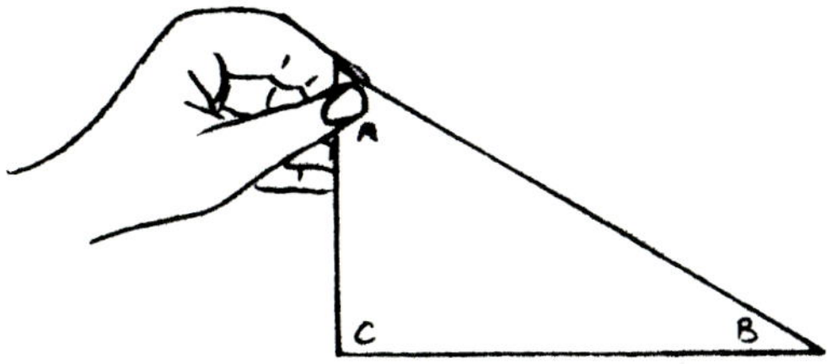

1 Cut a triangle of vegetable parchment paper and hold the shortest side closest to your wrist, point A on the diagram.

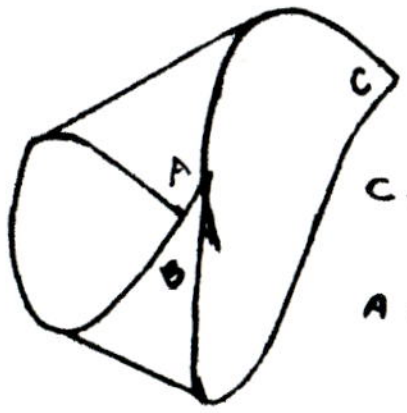

2 Take point B in the other hand, move it away from you, then up and over the back of the fingers holding point A.

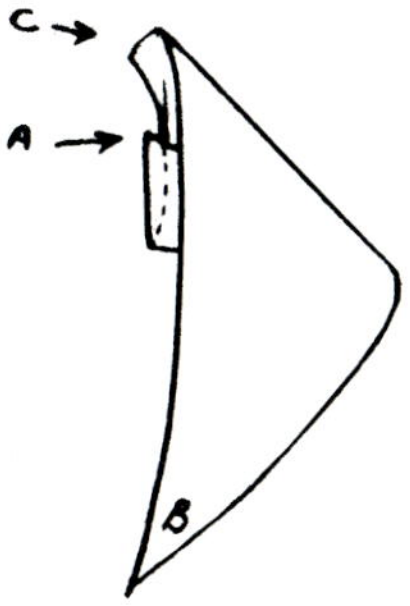

3 Draw point B steadily towards you and, at the same time, slide the edge of the paper under the thumb holding point A.

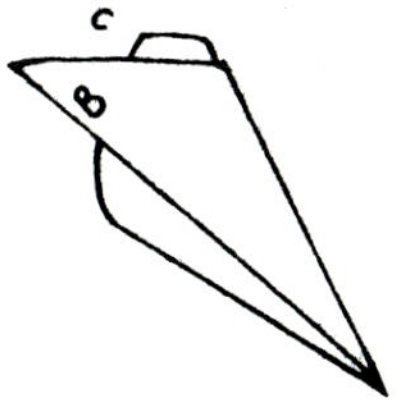

4 The cone will start to take shape; continue wrapping point B around it, keeping the paper taut.

5 This makes a cone with a sharp point. Change your grip and fold the loose ends of the parchment into the bag. Tear a small flap into the fold line to lock the layers of paper together.

To pipe a straight line, touch the point of the piping tube (tip) to the surface, then, keeping constant pressure , lift the bag and let the icing flow steadily. Keep the point of the tube (tip) about 5 cm (2 inch) above the surface. Neither squeeze the bag too hard nor pull at the icing, or the strand will snap.

Leaves are usually piped with a special piping tube (tip). Hold the bag at a 45 degree angle and squeeze it fairly hard at first, jiggling the bag at the same time. As each leaf begins to form, relax the pressure and withdraw the bag in one motion. This action pulls the icing into a point, forming the leaf tip.

It is important to control the rate at which the icing is squeezed out of the piping tube (tip). These stars are all made with a no. 7 star piping tube (tip). They show the difference made by varying the pressure. The bag is held in a vertical position when piping stars.

HANDY HINT

To pipe a circle around the perimeter of a round cake, place the cake on a turntable and, holding the piping tube (tip) steady, touch it to the surface of the cake to begin the line. Lift the bag as you begin to squeeze it and steadily rotate the turntable, holding the bag stationary.

PIPING VARIEGATED LEAVES

Try this technique to achieve an interesting and attractive colour variation for piped leaves. Before putting the icing into the bag, put a streak of yellow colour down one side of the bag and piping tube (tip), and a streak of dark green down the other side. Make sure the streaks of colour line up with the sides of the point of the piping tube (tip). Fill the bag with green icing, then when the leaves are piped, they will be tinged with lighter icing on one side and darker icing on the other side.

HANDY HINT

- *To check the consistency of icing, put a little in a bag and pipe a short row of shells, then examine them closely. After about 1 minute the icing should look dry, not shiny, and the ridges and grooves should be clean and sharp. If the icing seems too wet, add a little extra icing (confectioners') sugar to it and beat well.*
- *Another way of testing icing if you are using a fine piping tube (tip), is to pipe a strand between two fingers and then move your fingers apart slightly. If the loop breaks straight away, then the icing is too wet. If you have trouble piping the loop in the first place, the icing is too stiff, so add a few drops of water or egg white.*

FLOODING ICING

After you have thinned the icing, cover it and leave it to stand for a few minutes. Any air bubbles will rise to the surface and these can be dispersed by gently stirring the icing with a knife.

Shells vary in size according to the pressure applied. Hold the bag at an angle of 45 degrees to the surface and push out the icing to form the fattest part of the shell, then release the pressure on the bag, and pull the piping tube (tip) straight back. Place the piping tube (tip) directly behind the tail of the shell just piped and pipe another which covers its tail.

Scrolls are piped with a star piping tube (tip). To taper them, begin by squeezing the bag steadily while moving the point of the piping tube (tip) slowly. As you near the end of each scroll relax the pressure and increase the rate at which you move the bag. Practise piping scrolls in each direction so that you form 'C' and 'S' shapes.

FLOODING

This type of painting with icing is described as flooding, run-out work or run-in work. It is a very effective technique which can be employed to create detailed pictures in bold colours. Run-out or run-in designs are often piped onto waxed paper or on a teflon-coated non-stick mat, in which case an outline is piped first and then it is filled with thinned royal icing. Flooding is usually carried out directly on the iced surface without piping an outline.

Whichever method you use, the royal icing should have the same consistency. Make up fresh icing to normal piping consistency, then add water, a few drops at a time, and stir gently – do not beat the icing. To determine whether the icing is sufficiently runny, swirl it with a knife and count steadily to ten. After 10 seconds, the swirls should have subsided and the surface of the icing should be smooth again.

Piped outlines form a boundary to prevent the icing overflowing the edge of a design. The outlines should be piped using icing of a normal consistency and a no. 0 or no. 1 piping tube (tip). Flooding icing will form a skin very quickly, so have a brush ready to push it right up to the piped outlines. Also, use the brush to burst any air bubbles that may appear in the icing.

When creating a complicated design, work in different sections of the picture at the same time. It is important to avoid having two wet areas side by side, as one will bleed into the other. Shine an anglepoise lamp onto the design so that the icing dries while you work. The warmth will also help the icing to dry with a good shine.

These trees and parcels are piped onto a transparent teflon-coated mat with the design underneath. Pipe the outline first to prevent the icing flowing over the edge of the design edge. Then use a piping bag with a very small hole cut at the point of the bag.

With practice you can work directly onto a cake without a piped outline. Keep the piping tube (tip) point in the icing as it flows. Use a fine paintbrush to break air bubbles and to direct the icing. It only takes minutes for the icing to form a skin. Then you can fill neighbouring areas.

USING PASTILLAGE

Pastillage has many uses and most ornaments, sugar flowers and leaves are made using this versatile medium as there are many ways of enhancing its appearance with colours and glazing.

When you are actually working with the paste, temporarily store the pieces you intend to use in a polythene bag. When it is rolled very thin, pastillage dries within minutes, so immediately cover any rolled pieces which are not in use. I use a very thick piece of clear plastic material, my 'floppy mat', for this purpose.

Keep any unused paste in good condition by wrapping it in plastic wrap, then placing it in an airtight plastic container before putting it in the refrigerator. Most mixtures can be stored in this way for several weeks but it is important to knead them occasionally so that the paste retains its elasticity and malleability.

DUSTING WITH COLOUR

Dusting powder is used to achieve subtle gradations of colour on pastillage. Apply the powders to hardened paste using a fairly large brush. Stipple the colour on, working from the outside edge into the middle of the flower or leaf. Always work on a piece of kitchen roll or tissue as it is easier to clean up when you have finished. This technique is illustrated on page 46 for colouring the flame on the Holly Cake.

CUTTING PASTILLAGE

Thin sections of pastillage can be cut very accurately with a long-bladed knife. Use a guillotine action to cut the paste. Do not drag the tip of the blade through the paste as this causes it to stretch and distort.

MAKING PASTILLAGE LEAVES

1 To create realistic pastillage leaves, mark their surface by pressing them against a special veining tool while they are still soft. Cutters and tools for this purpose are available in plastic and metal, in a wide variety of shapes and patterns.

2 Leaves look best if they are allowed to harden into twisted and bent shapes. Drape the soft leaves over crinkled foil and leave them to harden. Then dip them in confectioners' glaze.

3 Confectioners' glaze is an edible varnish used to preserve sugar models. Holly leaves and seals from the cake on page 36 are shown here both before and after they have been glazed. Small items can be dipped into the bowl of glaze, while larger ones are usually painted with glaze.

FREEZING PASTILLAGE

You can freeze pastillage. Chop the paste into small cubes, coat each cube with white vegetable fat (shortening) and wrap it in plastic wrap. Seal the cubes in a freezer bag and freeze the paste. It keeps for up to a couple of years if well wrapped. When you want to use the paste, ensure that it is totally thawed before unwrapping it, otherwise it will become sticky.

BASIC MODELLING

The four basic shapes: ball, cone, pear and sausage.

If you have never tried modelling, why not make the simple animals and objects shown on the next few pages? Almost all of them are derived from four basic shapes – the ball, the cone, the pear and the sausage.

These four basic shapes are modelled by hand. Use the palms of the hands to roll ball shapes and the edges and sides of the hands to form the pear and cone. Roll the sausage shape on the worksurface to obtain an even result.

Although a set of modelling tools makes a very useful addition to the cake decorator's workbox, most of these figures can be made using only a craft knife and a pair of fine-pointed scissors.

Figures are often made to look comical by modelling their heads much larger in proportion to their bodies than they would be in the real world, and a ratio of 3:5 seems to work well in most cases. For example, if you make a figure with a head which weighs about 30g (1 oz), the main part of the body should weigh about 50g (1¾ oz). For more realistic models, or those formed in moulds, the proportions should be as close as possible to reality.

The simple shapes shown on the following pages are all made using a paste combining sugarpaste pastillage in equal quantities.

THE BALL

Shaping a ball is the most fundamental technique for all modelling as the action achieves a smooth surface on all sides of the paste. Place the paste between the palms of the hands and roll it strongly in a circular motion. Having achieved the basic shape, roll the paste more gently and uniformly, raising the hands to chin level. In this position the eye can follow the working of the paste and you will be able to see if there are any irregularities in the surface of the ball.

The ball is used for the heads of many of the models shown in this book. The basic steps are always similar. Use a dogbone modelling tool to make sockets for the eyes and a cone-shaped tool to make a socket for the nose. Then pipe the features. In this illustration, the head is enclosed in a hood of blue paste. Similar finished figures may be seen on pages 19, Father Christmas, and 33, eskimos.

Handy Hint

When making models with clothes, it is usually only necessary to make the head and the hands with realistic details, since the arms and legs will be concealed by the folds of the garments.

Facial Expressions

The eyes of the figures play an important role. Varying the position, both of the whites of the eyes and the pupils, can totally change the facial expressions.

THE CONE

Roll a ball in the palms of the hands to ensure that the surface is smooth, then turn the upper hand so that the edge of the palm is resting on one side of the ball. Slide the upper hand diagonally several times over the ball and it will form a cone. To elongate the cone, position it so that its point is between the heels of both hands and gently rub them together. This will cause the point of the cone to extend and become thinner.

Making Hands

One of the most widely used applications of the cone is for making hands.Take a small cone of paste and flatten the broad end. Use fine-pointed scissors to snip a V-shaped section out of one side to create a thumb. Make three small cuts to form the fingers. Do not make these cuts too deep, as the base of the fingers should extend only a little way beyond the tip of the thumb. Curve the fingers so that the hand appears relaxed.

THE PEAR

The pear shape is formed from a cone. Place the cone between the heels of the hands and adjust the position of the upper hand so that it is slightly higher on the cone, then rub it against the palm of the lower hand. This will cause the cone to bulge slightly. This basic pear shape can be elongated at either end using the same basic action to form all sorts of animal bodies.

THE SAUSAGE

As usual, start by modelling a ball to give the paste a smooth surface. If you try to roll the paste into a sausage between your hands, it becomes more of a cigar shape as it tends to become thicker in the middle and tapered at the ends. Roll the paste on the worksurface, making sure that you use the palm or heel of the hand rather than the fingers which make lumpy sausages as the paste is pressed into the spaces between the fingers.

A cone, when elongated, twisted into shape and finished with a modelling tool, becomes the head of a trumpeting elephant! The two-coloured ears are made by sticking thinly rolled grey and pink pastillage together. Stick them into position with gum arabic glue.

Two pear shapes form a polar bear. The larger pear forms the bear's body and the smaller one makes the head. The mouth is made by snipping the paste with scissors. Press tiny balls of paste into the soft head with a small ball tool to make ears. Model four small sausage shapes for legs. Use black icing to highlight the bear's features.

A tiny sausage of black paste assumes the shape of a seal when one end is split, then squeezed with a ridged modelling tool. Cut the front flippers by snipping the paste away from the body with scissors, bending the flippers forward. Indent the neck slightly and shape the nose to a blunt point.

HANDY HINT

When modelling objects which come in pairs, for example, hands, arms or legs, to overcome the difficulty of making them of equal size, roll a piece of paste into a sausage then cut it in half lengthways. Each piece may then be moulded to shape and the pair will match.

HANDY HINT

Make these toys as miniature models which can be positioned in a toy shop window as shown on page 76.

TOYS

All sorts of figures and toys can be made in a variety of sizes using the basic shapes.

BUS

Shape a rectangular block of red paste using a blunt knife and cut out the door at the back. Use tiny pieces of white or black paste for the windows, wheels, lights and radiator, and stick them in place with gum arabic glue, see page 9. Use a food colour pen to paint the markings on the windows and radiators.

YACHT

Roll out white pastillage and cut out two triangles for the sails, then leave them to dry for at least a few hours. Model a sausage and roll it to a point at each end, then flatten it along one side. Pinch out the opposite side to form the keel. Then stick the sails into the hull while the paste is still soft.

TRAIN

A toy train does not have to look like the real thing. Roll a sausage for the engine and a ball for the cab. Indent one side of the cab with a large ball tool to make it hollow, then cut the side shapes with a pair of fine-pointed scissors. Make a very small cone for the funnel and mark the wheels with a modelling knife. Pipe a red dot on the front of the engine and a pair of eyes on the front of the cab.

DOLL

This little rag doll is less than 10cm (4 inch) tall. Shape a cone for the body and split the pointed end into two using a sharp craft knife. Blue pastillage has been used for the clothing: roll the pastillage very thin and frill it, see page 20, before wrapping it around the body. Use a rectangle of blue paste for the bodice and add white strips of paste for the belt. Dress all the limbs before joining the arms and head to the torso. Use yellow paste for the hair.

EGG PEOPLE AND CHRISTMAS TREES

These ornaments are completely edible and simple to make. The trees are piped over wafer ice-cream cornets and the figures are all made on sugar-coated chocolate eggs. The garments on the figures are made from thinly rolled pastillage and they are attached with Gum Arabic Glue, see page 9. Larger pieces, such as the heads and the arms, can also be secured with gum arabic glue or with suitably coloured royal icing for extra strength. Some parts of the models have to be dry before the finishing touches can be added, so make them in stages over two or more days.

750g (1½ lb) Sugarpaste, see page 8
500g (1 lb) Pastillage, see page 10
red, blue, black, skintone, green, Cornish cream, dark brown and peach paste colours
4 sugar-coated chocolate eggs
250 g (8 oz/ 1 cup) Royal Icing, see page 9
Gum Arabic Glue, see page 9
3 ice-cream wafer cones
red, silver and gold coloured dragees (nonpareils)
rice paper

EQUIPMENT
fluted garrett frill cutter
baby face mould
set of modelling tools
10 and 7.5cm (4 and 3 inch) round cutters
nos. 51 and 52 leaf piping tubes (tips), no. 5 star piping tube (tip) and nos. 0, 1 and 2 writing tubes (tips)
piping bags
scriber
paintbrushes
small teardrop (rose petal) cutter
small blossom plunger cutter
jasmine cutter
cocktail stick (toothpick)
no. 30 mini single scallop crimper
small carnation or fluted cutter

Mix 440g (14 oz) each of sugarpaste and pastillage together and knead until thoroughly combined. Leave 250g (8 oz) paste white. Colour 90g (3 oz) paste black, 185g (6 oz) skintone, 155g (5 oz) blue and 185g (6 oz) red. Before starting any of the models, cut a circle or plaque of sugarpaste for each egg. Attach the eggs to the plaques with royal icing, placing the pointed ends up. Leave to set for 24 hours.

CHOIR BOY OR GIRL

Make the face and head in one piece by pressing a 60g (2 oz) ball of skintone paste into the lightly greased baby face mould. Model the back of the head by hand, then remove from the mould. Define the mouth, if necessary, with a small ball tool. Dry overnight.

Paint the features with food colour using a fine paint-brush. Then pipe the hair using a no.1 piping tube (tip) with brown royal icing. Swirl the icing with a dampened brush to fill in any gaps. Leave to dry for about 1 hour.

Use a small rose petal cutter to cut out shoes from black paste and stick them to the plaque. Indent the shoes with the rose petal cutter to form the toe caps and mark holes for laces using the cone modelling tool. Cut a small rectangle of black paste for the book and support it in the open shape. Dry on wax paper.

Roll out blue paste to make the surplice and cut a 10cm (4 inch) circle. Paint the top of the egg with gum arabic glue and drape the paste centrally over it. Use a garrett frill cutter to cut out a scalloped circle of paste and use the small blossom plunger cutter to mark the scalloped edge to create a lacy effect, then drape this over the surplice, sticking it in place with gum arabic glue. Make two pleats to give the impression that the figure has outstretched arms beneath the cape.

Cut a small star with the jasmine cutter and stick this to the top of the egg. Then stick the head in position with royal icing, hiding any excess icing by lifting the points of the star to form a collar. Make the pages of the book by rolling out a very thin rectangle of white paste and sticking it into the black cover. Support the book in front of the choir boy on a foam pad, then use a no. 2 piping tube (tip) and skintone royal icing to pipe the hands. Once dry, the icing will hold the book in place.

ANGEL

Make a head as for the choir boy but do not mark the open mouth. Pipe the hair using a no. 0 piping tube (tip) and yellow royal icing, squeezing it onto the head from a distance of 1cm (½ inch) so that it drops in loops and curls. While the icing is still wet, cut a halo from a circle of rice paper and stick it to the back of the head.

Cut a 12cm (4.5 inch) circle of paste for the dress and frill it with a cocktail stick (toothpick), see below. Use a no.30 mini single scallop crimper to decorate the edge above the frill, then drape the dress over the egg, securing it with gum arabic glue.

Make the arms and sleeves in one piece from a sausage of white paste measuring about 12cm (4½ inch) long. Use a cone modelling tool to open the cuffs, then frill the

MAKING A FRILL Frilling is a basic decorating skill which is much easier than it looks. Use a fluted cutter to stamp out the circle. Place a cocktail stick (toothpick) on the edge of the paste, then, while pressing the stick with a finger, roll it around the perimeter. This action stretches small areas of the paste, causing it to pucker behind the cocktail stick and so creating the frill.

edge of the paste with a cocktail stick (toothpick). Mould the hands, see page 17 and set them into the sleeves with gum arabic glue, then drape the arms around the top of the egg, securing with gum arabic glue.

Cut out a small scalloped circle using the carnation cutter and frill the edges. Glue this to the top of the egg and pipe some royal icing on it, then attach the head. Disguise the join by lifting the edge of the frill.

Pipe a strand of royal icing between the two hands using a no. 2 piping tube (tip) and stick gold and silver dragees onto it while the icing is still wet. For the finishing touch, add a pair of rice-paper wings.

FATHER CHRISTMAS

Start with the head, see page 16, as this needs to dry before putting the hat on. Take a 60g (2 oz) ball of skin-tone paste and indent two impressions for eyes. Use the pointed cone tool to make a hole just below the eyes for the nose. To make the nose, roll a tiny amount of paste into a cone. Use gum arabic glue to stick it in place. Allow the head to dry.

To make the boots, roll two pea-sized balls of black paste into cones. Place the point of each cone against the side of the egg and stick them in place. For the hands, take a ball of black paste about the size of a hazelnut and shape it so that it tapers to a point at each end. Use the blade of the modelling tool to mark a zig-zag pattern down the middle, then bend the pointed ends into a 'U' shape – almost like a pair of horns.

continued overleaf

Angel Wings

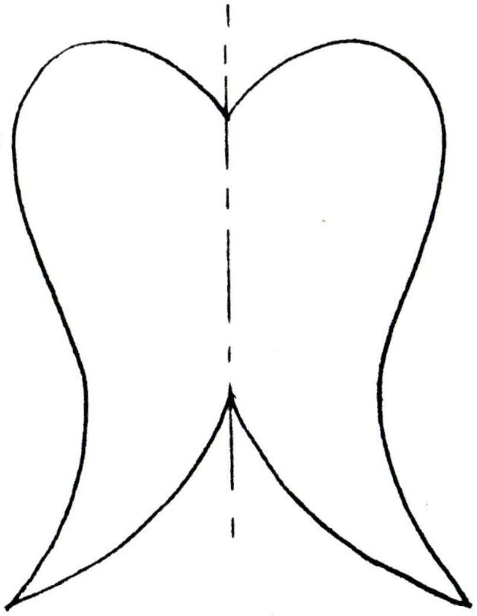

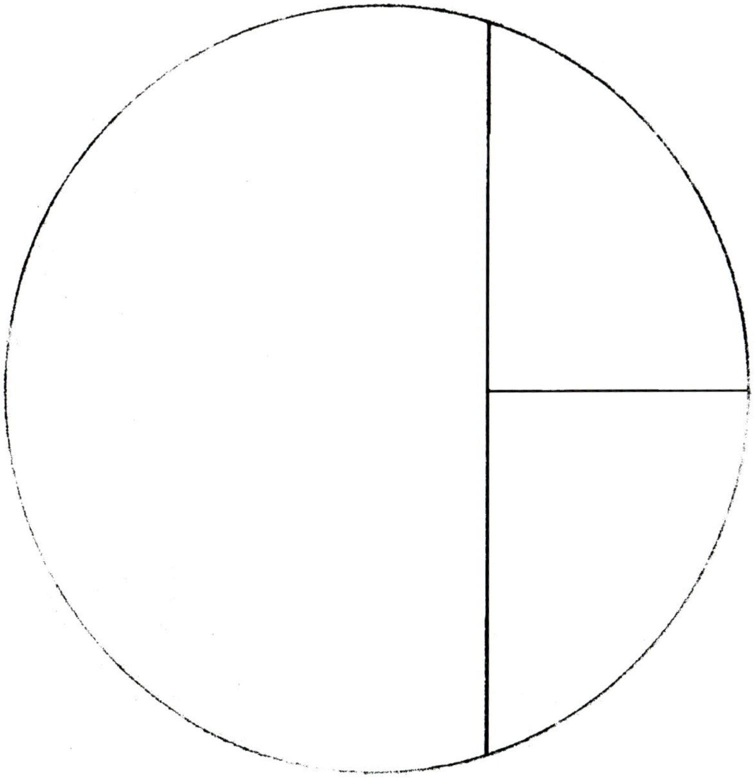

Halo

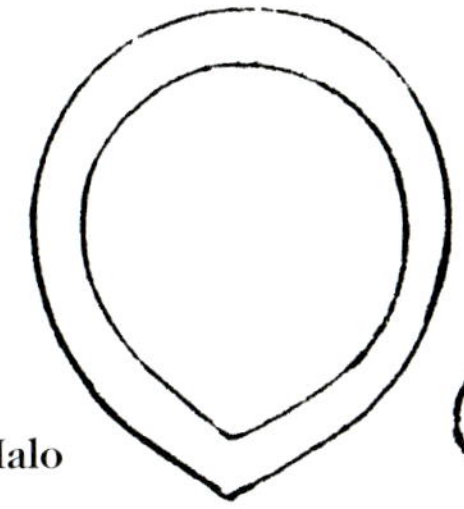

Angel's Neck Ruffle

Father Christmas' Coat

To make the coat, roll out the red paste. Cut out a 10cm (4 inch) and a 7.5cm (3 inch) circle. Then cut the larger circle as shown in the diagram, see page 21, to form the two sleeves and the coat. Paint some gum arabic glue along the edge of the larger section and drape this around the egg, overlapping the gummed edges at the front. To make the sleeves, roll the remaining sections into two cones and stick them into position with the pointed ends meeting on top of the egg. Trim the edges of the coat by using a no. 5 star piping tube (tip) to pipe a line of stiff royal icing. Stick the hands in position with the pointed ends inside each sleeve

Cut the smaller circle of red paste in half and roll one piece into a cone to make a hat. Then stick it onto the back of the head. Pipe some royal icing on the top of the egg to attach the head. Fill the eye sockets with white royal icing and leave to dry, then paint the eyeballs with black colour. Pipe the beard and moustache in white royal icing using a no. 5 star piping tube (tip).

SNOWMAN

Roll 60g (2 oz) white paste into a ball to form the head. Make two eye sockets and a hole for the nose. Use a U-shaped tool to mark the mouth. Colour a tiny amount of white paste bright orange and roll it into a carrot shape to make the nose. Attach it with gum arabic glue. Leave the head to dry.

Make the arms by rolling a sausage of paste, then cut it in half lengthways. Roll each piece to form an elongated cone and stick them to the egg with the pointed ends meeting on the top. Attach the head to the egg with royal icing. Fill the eye sockets with white royal icing and leave to dry.

To make the hat, roll a pea-sized ball of black paste and mark the centre using the blade modelling tool. Roll out a circle of black paste and stick the ball of paste on top. Stick this hat to the head with gum arabic glue

The scarf is made from separate strands of blue, red and white paste which are twisted together to form a spiral. Flatten the spiral with a mini rolling pin, then roll it out so that the paste is quite thin. Trim the edges and cut the fringe with a sharp knife.

Finish by piping three or four buttons down the snowman's front using a no. 1 writing tube (tip) with black royal icing and pipe two black dots for the eyes .

CHRISTMAS TREES

Cut a circle of green pastillage the same size as the base of the ice-cream wafer cone. Attach the paste to the cone with green royal icing.

Model the tree trunk with brown pastillage and roughen it with a scriber so that it looks like bark. Then trim it to about 2.5cm (1 inch) long and attach it to the pastillage on the base of the cone with a little royal icing. Leave to dry overnight.

Using a no. 52 leaf piping tube (tip) and starting at the base of the cone, pipe a row of leaves. The second and subsequent rows of leaves are arranged so that the tips of the upper leaves fall between the tips of those in the row below. Two-thirds of the way up the cone, change to a smaller no. 51 leaf piping tube (tip) to complete the tree. Leave to dry.

Once the leaves are dry, the trees can by decorated with coloured dragees or dusted with icing (confectioners') sugar.

HANDY HINT

Make the snowman's scarf in the colours of an appropriate local sports club.

CHRISTMAS TREES IN TUBS

The Christmas trees can be set into red tubs made of sugar-paste or pastillage.

CAKE DESIGNS

Making and decorating a cake is an essential preparation for the festive season. Wherever I am, the traditional images conjured up at Christmas time are broadly similar - peace, goodwill, comfort and relaxation. Few aspects combine these ideas better than Christmas cake, freshly baked, still hot from the oven and imparting a spicy, aromatic warmth. So, when the stores are noisy and crowded, there is nothing I like better than to settle down quietly at home to decorate my family's Christmas cake. I hope to share some of this pleasure with you in the designs which follow. Happy Christmas!

EQUIPMENT

Clockwise from bottom left:
large holly cutter; rolling pin; modelling sticks; bought holly berries; large scallop crimper; small crimping tools; piping bags; piping tubes (tips); scraper; straight edge; scriber; round cutters; calyx cutter; set of poinsettia cutters; holly leaf cutters and all-in-one flower cutter; gold and silver dragees (nonpareils); smoother; paintbrushes; cranked palette knife; semi-transparent, non-stick, floppy mat; on the mat: straight frill cutter, circular garrett frill cutter and a set of modelling tools; leaf veiners.

TEMPLATES

FOR QUICK AND EASY CAKES

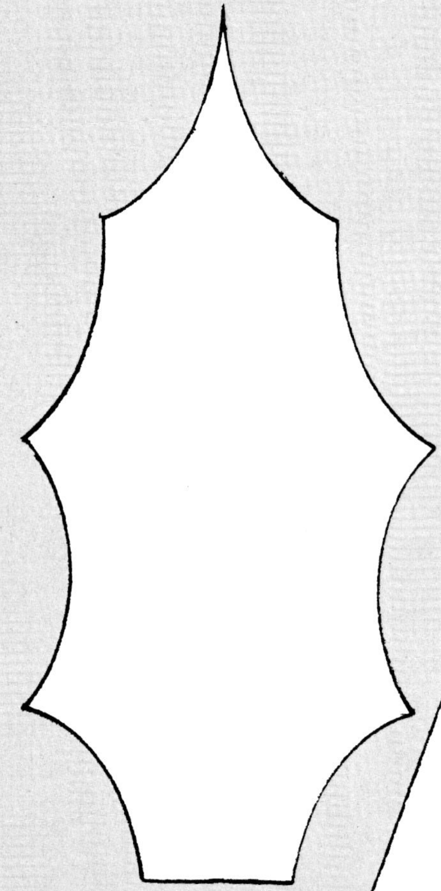

Holly Cake, see page 46

Candle Flame

Christmas at the Pole, see page 36

Iceberg Sections

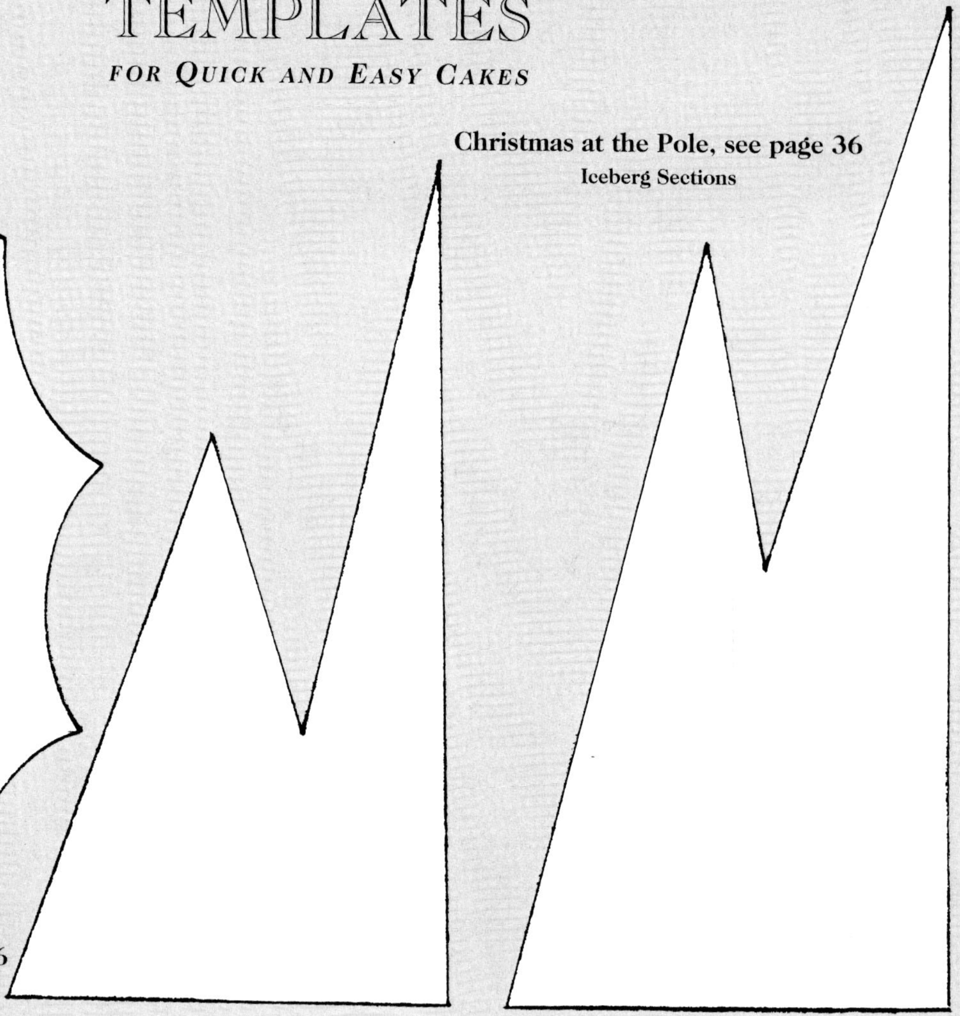

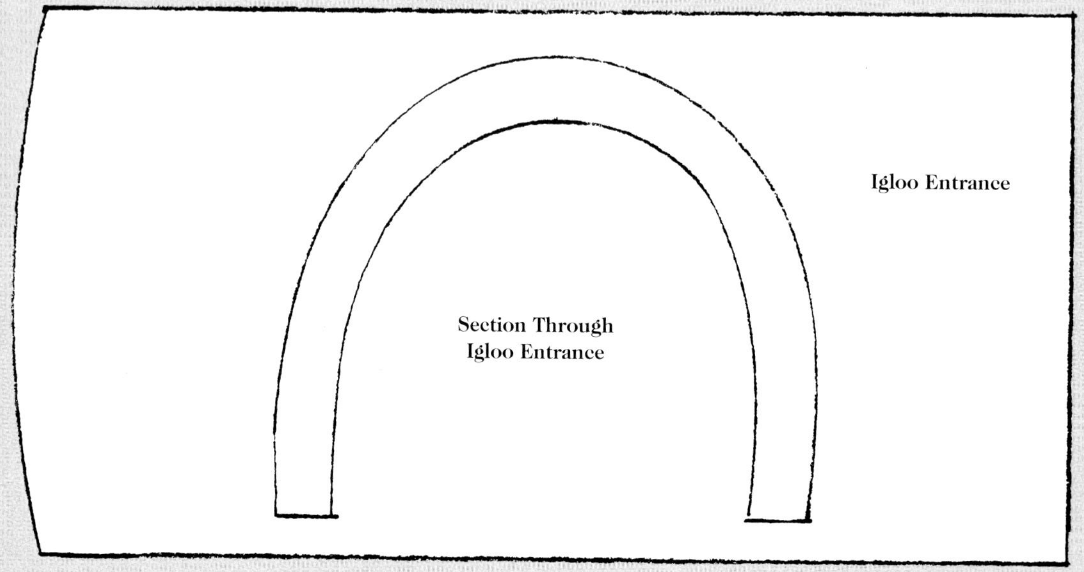

Merry-Making Robins, see page 38

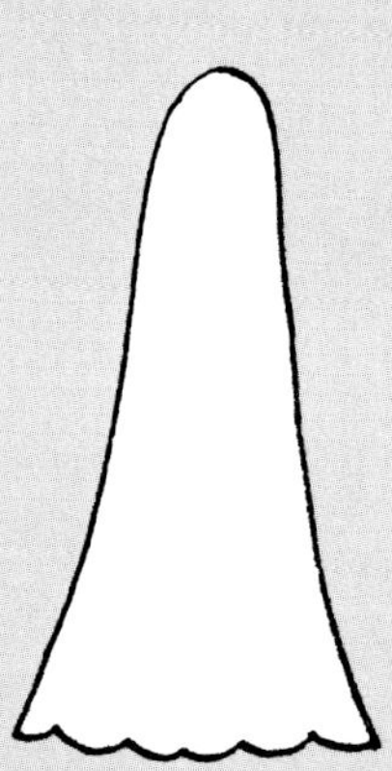

Bird's Tail

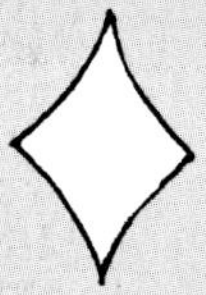

Bird's Beak

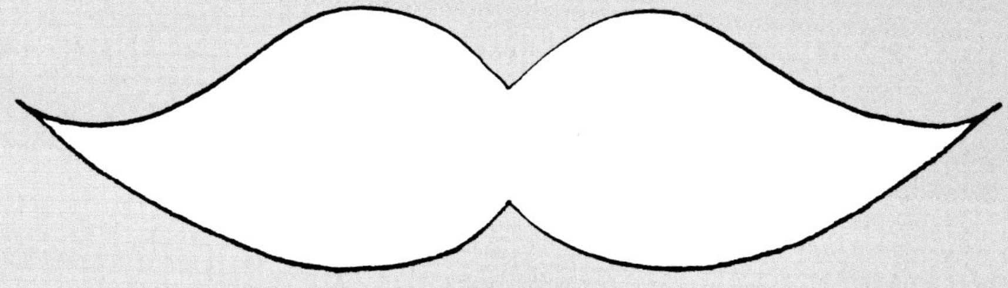

Bird's Wings

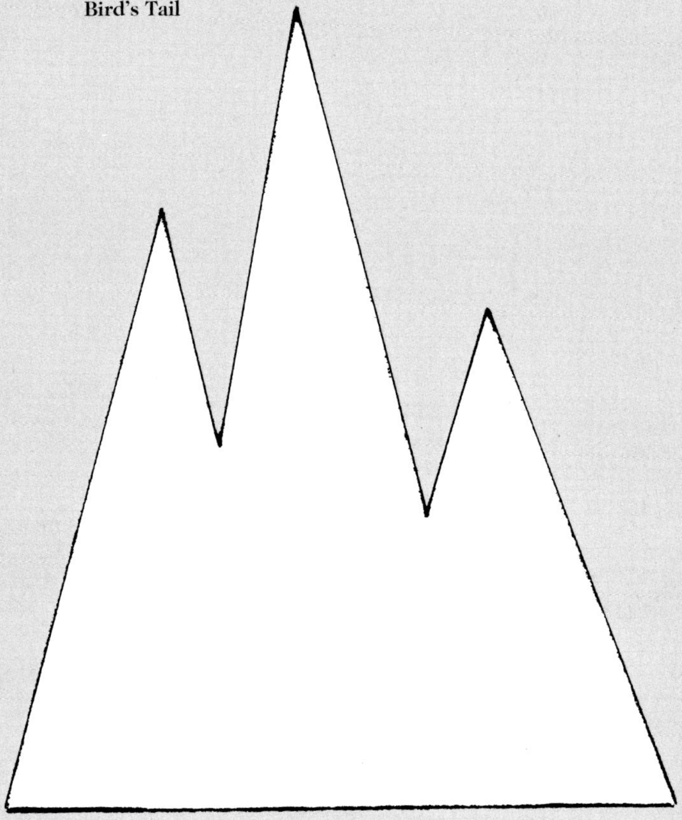

Christmas at The Pole, see page 36

Iceberg Section

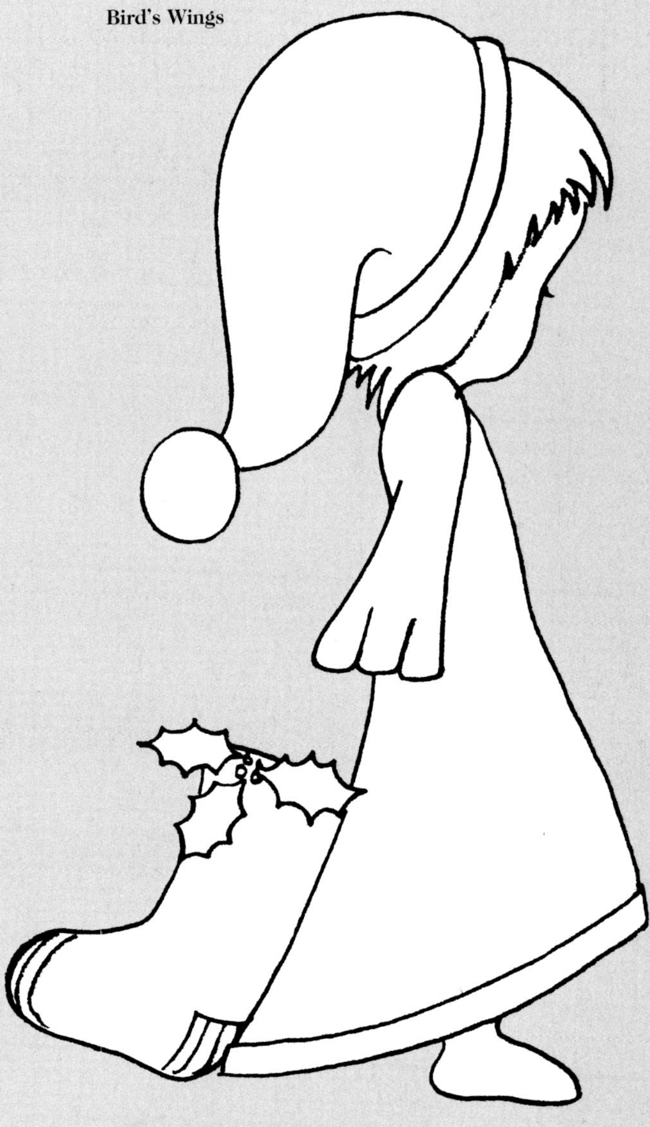

Merry Christmas Cake, see page 42

Run-out Design for Cake Top

Gingerbread Sleigh, see page 34

NOTE These patterns must be enlarged by 133% on a photocopier

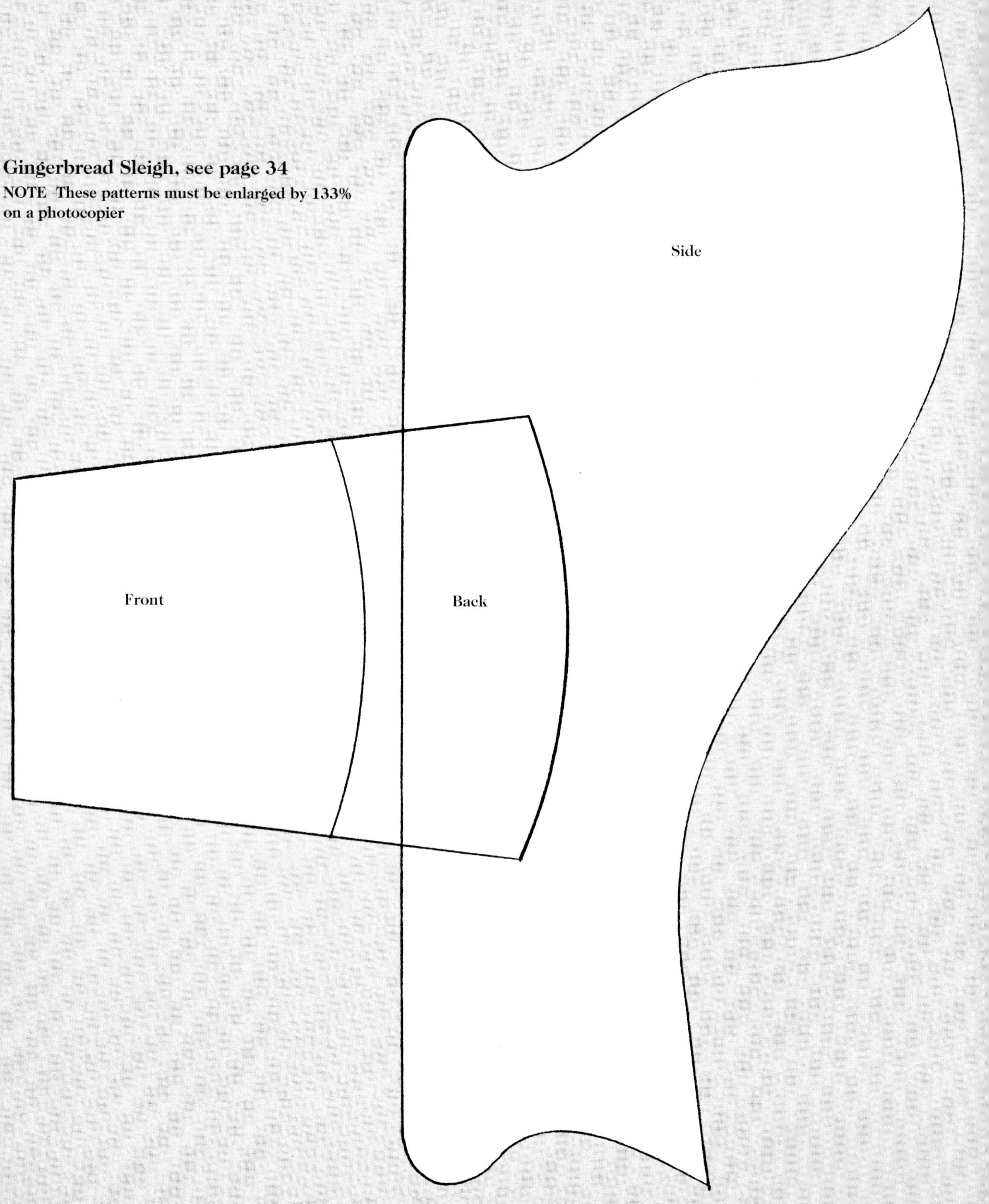

Santa Cake, see page 28

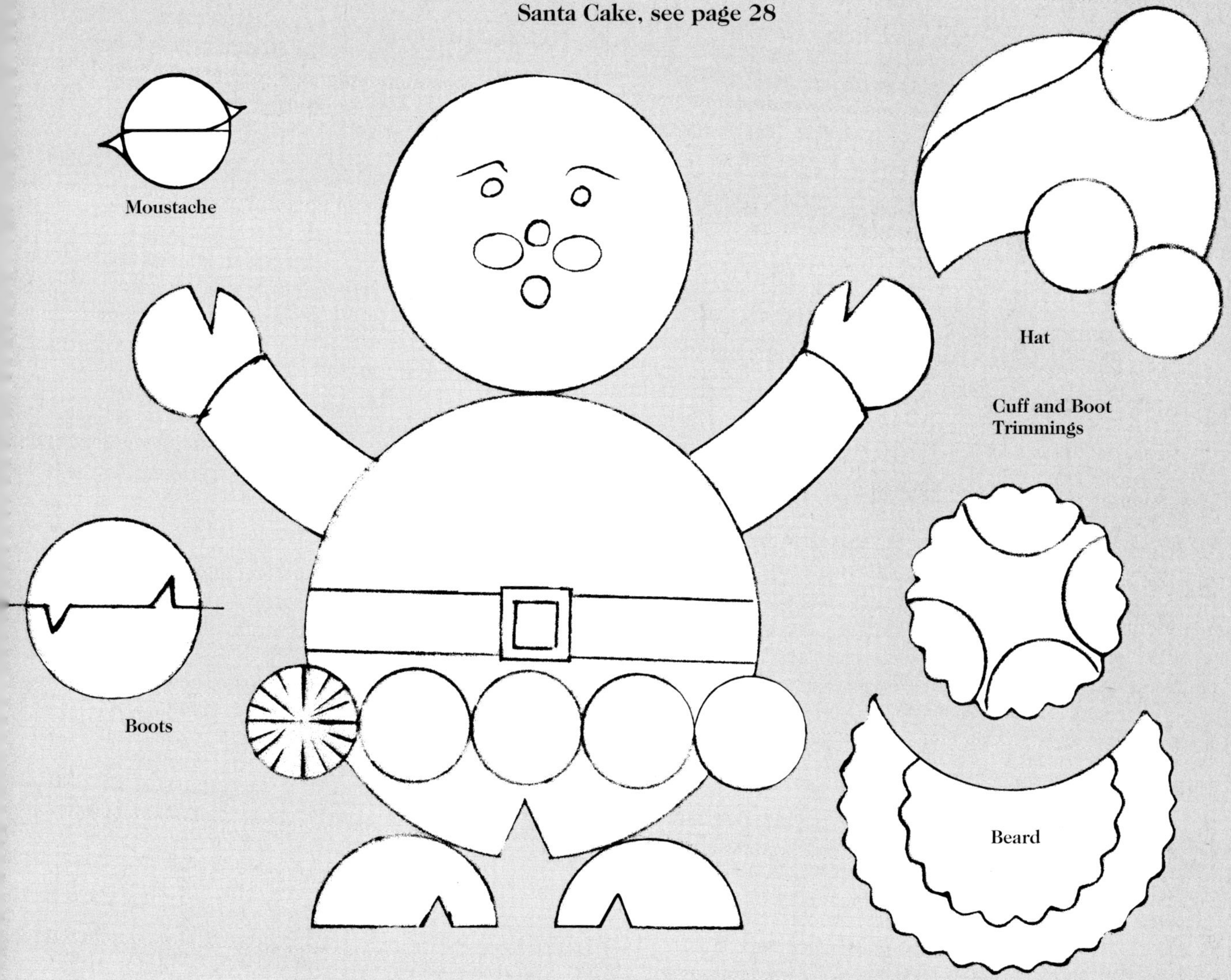

Gingerbread Sleigh, see page 34

NOTE This template must be enlarged by 133% on a photocopier

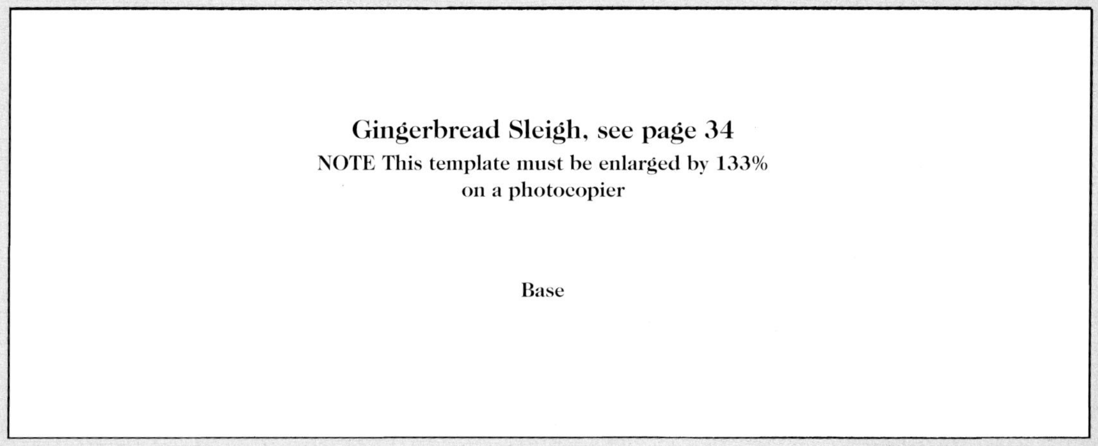

SANTA CAKE

A royal-iced cake with shell piping and a Santa Claus cut from coloured sugarpaste makes this striking design. A bow of wide, floppy velvet ribbon adds a touch of luxury.

20cm (8 inch) round fruit cake, see page 7
875g (1¾ lb) Marzipan (almond paste), see page 8
500g (1 lb/2 cups) Royal Icing, see page 9
375g (12 oz) Sugarpaste or Marzipan (almond paste), see pages 8 and 9
red, black and skintone paste food colours

EQUIPMENT

28cm (11 inch) round cake board
no. 6 shell piping tube (tip)
large piping bags
set of 1 – 7cm (½ – 3 inch) round cutters
set of 4.5 – 6cm (1½ – 2½ inch) scalloped round cutters
1.5 metres (1⅔ yd) red velvet ribbon

Cover the cake and board with marzipan (almond paste) and three layers of white royal icing. Leave to dry. Using the no. 6 shell piping tube (tip) and large piping bag filled with stiff royal icing, pipe a shell border around the top and bottom edges of the cake. Then leave to dry.

Santa Claus can be cut out of almond paste or sugarpaste. Colour 30g (1 oz) black, 60g (2 oz) skintone, 155g (5 oz) red and leave the remaining 125g (4 oz) white. Start by rolling out the red paste for the body. Cut a 7.5cm (3 inch) circle, then remove a 'V' shape section from the lower edge. Dampen the back of the circle with a little water and place it in the centre of the cake. Use the template on page 26 as a guide. Cut the arms and the hat and place them in the 10.00 and 2.00 o'clock positions.

Cut the cap from a 5cm (2 inch) circle of red paste and cut out a piece so that it fits against the top of the head. Set the cap aside until the face has been positioned. Roll out some black paste and cut a strip measuring 5mm (¼ inch) wide and 7.5cm (3 inch) long. Dampen this and place it in position to form the belt. Cut a small square to form the buckle.

To make the boots, cut a 2.5cm (1 inch) circle of black paste. Cut it in half and remove a small 'V' shape to fashion the sole and heel of each boot. Dampen the backs of the boots and position them about 5mm (¼ inch) below the body and about 1cm (½ inch) apart.

For the face, roll two very small balls of skintone paste to form the cheeks and place these on the cake about 2cm (¾ inch) above the body. Now roll out the rest of the skintone paste, cut out a 5cm (2 inch) circle and smooth it over the cheeks. The nose and mouth are just small balls of skintone and red paste, squashed slightly as they are stuck in place. Indent the mouth with the end of a paintbrush. Add two tiny balls of black paste for the eyes and tiny cigar-shaped rolls of white paste for the eyebrows.

Cut two 2cm (¾ inch) circles to form the hands. Follow the template to make the hands and stick them in place. Then build up the beard from white sugarpaste, cut with fluted cutters. Dampen the first, larger, layer of beard and place it over the lower portion of the face, then stick the smaller beard shape on top. Make the moustache from two semi-circles of paste.

Cut out 15 tiny circles and mark each with a star pattern, then use to trim the cap, coat and boots. Finally, cut another scalloped circle and use a small round cutter to cut out four sections to trim the cuffs and boots. Tie a bow of velvet ribbon around the cake.

YULE LOG

A yule log is made from a Swiss (jelly) roll and coated with chocolate buttercream. For extra effect, this one is decorated with meringue mushrooms and trailing ivy.

1 egg white
60g (2 oz/¼ cup) caster (superfine) sugar
30 x 20cm (12 x 8 inch) Swiss (Jelly) Roll, see page 4
315g (10 oz/1½ cups) American Buttercream, see page 9
1 tablespoon cocoa powder (unsweetened cocoa powder) or 2 tablespoons drinking chocolate powder plus extra for decorating
3 tablespoons chocolate liqueur or rum (optional)
brown and green paste food colours
60g (2 oz) Marzipan (almond paste), see page 8
icing (confectioners') sugar for decorating

EQUIPMENT

non-stick baking sheet
large fabric piping bag
large plain savoy piping tube (tip)
23 x 10cm (9 x 4 inch) log card
set of 3 ivy leaf cutters

Preheat the oven to 110°C(225°F/Gas ¼.) Make the meringue mushrooms by whisking the egg white until it stands in stiff peaks. Add half the sugar and whisk until the mixture is smooth and shiny. Using a large metal spoon, gently fold in the remaining sugar in two stages.

Put the meringue mixture into a large piping bag fitted with a savoy tube (tip) and pipe rounds of meringue in two sizes onto a non-stick baking sheet. Pipe small rounds for the stems and larger ones for the caps. The meringue will expand slightly as it cooks, so do not make the rounds too big. Bake the meringues for about 1 hour, until crisp and dry. Cool on a wire rack.

Reserve 60g (2 oz/generous ⅓ cup) of the buttercream. Beat the cocoa powder (unsweetened cocoa powder) or drinking chocolate powder into the rest of the buttercream and flavour it with 1 tablespoon of the chocolate liqueur or rum if liked.

Carefully unroll the cooled cake and remove the paper. Brush the cake with the remaining chocolate liqueur or rum, then spread with the chocolate buttercream and roll it up again.

Use some of the white buttercream to cover the ends of the log and spread the remainder over the log card. Use a flat-bladed knife to spread the remaining chocolate buttercream over the surface of the log and place it on the prepared card. Use brown food colour to paint the rings on the ends of the log.

Stick the caps of the mushrooms to the stalks with white buttercream and sift a little cocoa powder or drinking chocolate powder over them. Place them in position.

Colour the marzipan (almond paste) green and roll out a thin strand to form the ivy stem. Lay this over the log. Cut out about eight ivy leaves of different sizes, bend them into shape and place them against the stem. Finally, sift some icing (confectioners') sugar over the cake to give the impression of a fine dusting of snow.

VARIATIONS

The Swiss (jelly) roll may be flavoured as follows.

CHOCOLATE Add 15g (½ oz/2 tablespoons) cocoa powder (unsweetened cocoa powder) or 60g (2 oz/2 squares) grated plain (dark) chocolate to the flour.

HAZELNUT Add 30g (1 oz) ground hazelnuts to the flour.

GINGER Add 2 teaspoons ground ginger to the flour.

CITRUS Add 2 teaspoons grated orange, lemon or lime rind to the sugar.

1 2

ROLLING A SWISS (JELLY) ROLL

1 Lay non-stick paper on a dampened tea-towel and sprinkle with caster (superfine) sugar. Immediately the sponge is cooked, turn it out onto the paper. Trim the cake edges and make a shallow cut 2.5cm (1 inch) in from the shorter end.

2 Lay non-stick paper over the sponge. Start rolling up the cake at the cut end, keeping the paper inside it. Use the tea-towel and sugared paper to lift the cake .

HANDY HINT

It is important to work quickly when rolling a sponge as delay allows the sponge to settle, then it cracks when rolled.

ALPINE WINTER FUN

This cake is so easy to make and it is a great favourite with the children. White buttercream and a selection of commercial cake decorations transform a bell-shaped sponge cake into a winter playground. The Dolly Varden tin (pan) is also known as a tiffin or bell tin (pan).

TRIMMING THE CAKE

When the bell-shaped cake has cooled, replace it in its tin and use the rim of the tin as a guide when trimming any excess risen cake in order to obtain a flat top to make an even base when the cake is turned out again.

double quantity Sponge Cake, see page 4
20cm (8 inch) round Sponge Cake, see page 4
double quantity American Buttercream, see page 9

EQUIPMENT

large Dolly Varden tin (pan)
28 cm (11 inch) round cake board
selection of commercial decorations, for example 12 Christmas trees, 4 snowmen in different positions, Father Christmas, reindeer and 4 snow children
10cm (4 inch) palette knife or flat-bladed knife

Preheat the oven to 160°C(325°F/Gas 3). Grease and flour the Dolly Varden tin (pan). Turn the sponge cake mixture into the tin and bake for about 1½ hours, until a skewer inserted in the centre of the cake comes out clean. Turn the cake out of the tin and leave to cool on a wire rack.

Slice the round cake into two layers and cut these into spirals, see diagram. Brush the bell-shaped cake with warmed sieved apricot jam or spread it with buttercream and jam. Make sure the buttercream is well whisked. Beginning at the base of the cake, spread a thin layer of buttercream over the surface using a palette knife. Attach a spiral of sponge cake as shown below. Then brush the spiral of cake with warmed sieved apricot jam and a thin layer of buttercream.

Place the cake in the freezer for 1 hour or in the refrigerator for 2 hours. Then apply a more generous layer of buttercream, forming it into irregular peaks. Finish the coating on the slide by warming the knife in a bowl of hot water and wiping it along the area to be smoothed. Arrange a selection of bought decorations on the icing.

Cutting the layers of sponge cake into spiral strips: start at the outer edge and work towards the middle of the cake, keeping the strip as even in width as possible.

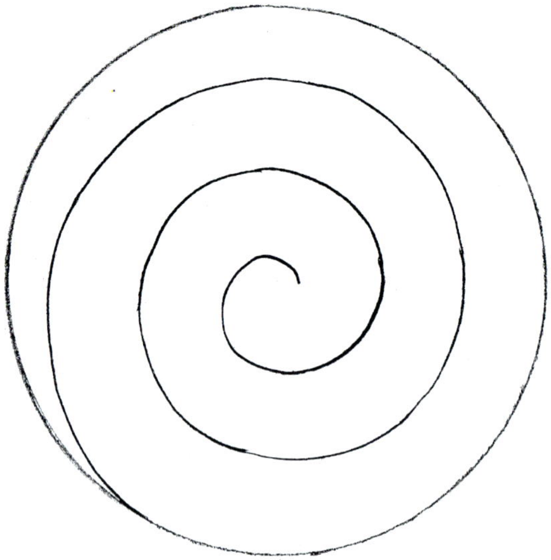

ATTACHING THE SPIRALS OF CAKE TO THE BELL-SHAPED CAKE
Slice the round cake horizontally into two 2.5cm (1 inch) thick layers. Cut both layers into spiral strips, see diagram. Then attach them around the bell-shaped cake, starting at the bottom and working up to the top.

HANDY HINT

If you need to keep the cakes overnight before decorating them, place them in a large plastic bag, then put them in the refrigerator.

GINGERBREAD SLEIGH

An edible gingerbread sleigh filled with sweets is an irresistible and inexpensive decoration at Christmas. Remember to keep filling it up with sweets, otherwise the sleigh itself will also be eaten by Boxing Day.

1 quantity Gingerbread, see page 6
500g (1 lb/2 cups) Royal Icing, see page 9
40 glazed holly leaves, see page 15
red and green paste food colours
selection of sweets

EQUIPMENT

scriber
large and small piping bags
no. 12 star piping tube (tip)
no. 1 piping tube (tip)

Preheat the oven to 190°C(375°F/Gas 5). Grease two baking sheets. Make the gingerbread, then roll it out to a thickness of 5mm (¼ inch) and cut out the pieces using the templates on pages 26 and 27. Turn the pattern over when cutting the sleigh's second side. Place the gingerbread on the baking sheets and bake for about 10 minutes, until evenly browned.

While the gingerbread is still hot, lay the templates over the appropriate pieces and trim them with a sharp knife. Do not wait until they are cold, as they become too crisp to cut easily. Allow the gingerbread to harden for 24 hours.

Using a scriber, mark the approximate positions for the icing garlands on the sides of the sleigh. Have something ready to support each side piece until the entire sleigh is assembled. Using a no. 12 star piping tube (tip), pipe a line of icing along one upper edge of the base and press one of the side pieces onto it. Next add the back panel: pipe some icing down one edge and along the bottom, then press it against the side panel and the base. Add the front panel in the same way and, lastly, add the second side. Pipe shells along each of the joins, both inside and out, to reinforce and embellish them.

When the sleigh has set, pipe the icing garlands on the marked side panels. The top edges are decorated with a heavier piped pattern, so exert a little more pressure on the piping bag. While the icing is still soft, stick the holly leaves in position. Let the icing dry before using a no. 1 piping tube (tip) and red icing to pipe holly berries.

Fill with a variety of sweets, chocolates, after-dinner mints, marzipan fruits or even little individual presents. Display the sleigh on a doily or wooden board.

HANDY HINT

Strong colours bleed into wet icing, so it is best to pipe the red holly berries after the garlands of white icing have set.

ASSEMBLING THE GINGERBREAD SLEIGH
Pipe a line of icing right around the edge of the three standing pieces and add the final panel. Remove any icing that has been squeezed from the joins.

CHRISTMAS AT THE POLE

Seals and icebergs, polar bears and Christmas presents complete a novelty cake which is very simple to decorate. The cake is baked in a dome-shaped tin (pan): a partially filled Dolly Varden, tiffin or bell tin (pan) is suitable, or half of a spherical Christmas pudding tin (pan) may be used. If you are really stuck, then use an ovenproof pudding basin.

2kg (4 lb) dome-shaped cake
750g (1½ lb) Marzipan (almond paste), see page 8
2kg (4 lb) Sugarpaste, see page 8
250g (8 oz) Pastillage, see page 10
125g (4 oz/½ cup) Royal Icing, see page 9
black, blue, red, pink, green and yellow paste food colours
3 holly leaves, see page 15
about 1 tablespoons piping gel

EQUIPMENT

set of modelling tools
small glass jar or suitable container for setting igloo tunnel
36cm (14 inch) oval cake board
no. 10 S-shaped crimper
large knife
1 cocktail stick (toothpick)
strand of covered wire or cotton
3.5cm (1½ inch) round cutter

Cover the cake with marzipan (almond paste) and sugarpaste. Cut the entrance tunnel in sugarpaste using the pattern on page 24 and lay this over a suitable jar as shown below. Then leave to dry overnight.

Set aside 250g (8 oz) sugarpaste to make the figures and cover the cake board with the remaining paste. Use the S-shaped crimper to crimp around the edge of the board. Place the cake towards the edge of the cake board, in order to leave room for the pastillage models, and use the 3.5cm (1½ inch) round cutter to cut out a circle of paste, about 7.5cm (3 inch) away from the front of the igloo. Place the entrance tunnel on the igloo. Use the royal icing to rough ice the board.

Roll the white pastillage to a thickness of 2.5mm (⅛ inch) and use a large knife to cut out the icebergs following the pattern on pages 24 and 25. Leave the icebergs to dry overnight. Cut out a thin circle of pastillage to fit the hole in the paste covering the board; paint it mottled blue and put it in the fishing hole. Mix any remaining pastillage with the sugarpaste for modelling the figures following the methods shown on pages 16 and 17.

Use royal icing to conceal the join between the igloo and its entrance tunnel, which can be festooned with sugar icicles, holly leaves and berries. Place the figures in position. The eskimo on the left is fishing for presents through a hole in the ice. A cocktail stick (toothpick) and covered wire or cotton thread make up his fishing rod. Cover the blue circle with a small quantity of piping gel to give the impression that there is water in the hole.

1

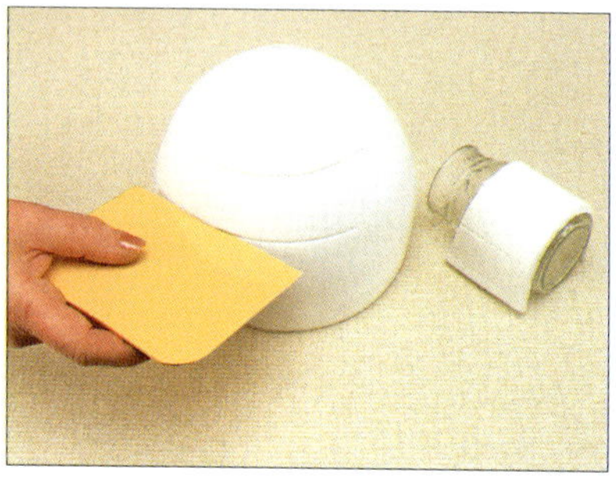

2

1 Before the paste covering hardens, indent the lines. Use a scraper for horizontal lines, and a modelling tool for vertical lines. The entrance tunnel is dried over a glass jar.
2 The eskimo's legs are made from a U-shaped piece of red paste tapered at each end. The torso and hood are made from blue paste. The hands are formed like mittens. The wrists fit into the hollowed ends of each arm. Long strips of paste trim the clothing edges.

MERRY-MAKING ROBINS

These little creatures have become thoroughly involved with the festive spirit. I think that the conventional robin-on-a-log cake is in need of a fresh interpretation, and this particular cake appeals greatly to inveterate party-goers.

18cm (7 inch) round fruit cake
1kg (2 lb) Marzipan (almond paste), see page 8
red, dark brown, chestnut, black, Cornish cream and green paste food colours
500g (1 lb/2 cups) Royal Icing, see page 9
icing (confectioners') sugar
125g (4 oz) Pastillage, see page 10
gold food paint
3 holly leaves, see page 15

EQUIPMENT

30cm (12 inch) round cake board
sieve • paintbrushes
scriber • fine-pointed scissors
modelling sticks or cocktail sticks (toothpicks)

Cover the cake with marzipan, reserving all the trimmings. Leave to dry for 1 – 2 days. Brush the top of the cake with boiled water or alcohol and follow step 1, below, for applying the top covering. Place it on the board and wrap a thick sausage of leftover marzipan from the top around the bottom edge. Colour 250g (8 oz/1 cup) royal icing dark brown and rough ice the side of the cake, texturing the wet icing with a fork to create the bark-like effect.

When the brown icing has dried, carefully rough ice the rest of the board with white royal icing. Thin the rest of the white icing with water until it has the consistency of thick cream and pour this over the top of the log to represent snow. Sprinkle the sides of the cake with a little sifted icing (confectioners') sugar.

Roll out a small rectangle of pastillage, then roll each end over a cocktail stick to form the scroll and set this aside to dry. Mix any scraps of marzipan with the rest of the pastillage and colour small amounts red, yellow and green. Divide the rest in half and colour one half light brown and the other half chestnut.

Make all the birds from similar pieces, following the patterns for the wings, tail and beaks on page 25, and step 2, below. Flatten a small amount of red paste on top of a walnut-sized piece of light-brown paste and roll together. Mark the bodies with a scriber and make tiny sausages, about 2.5cm (1 inch) long, for legs. Mould a pear-shaped head, then squeeze slightly to flatten the narrow end. Indent the eyes. Snip out a crown of feathers on the top and two feathers on the fattest part of the cheeks. Use the very small plastic modelling stick or cocktail stick (toothpick) to indent the feather pattern on the wings.

Fill the eye sockets with white royal icing and dry. Paint the faces carefully so that their expressions are different. Paint the eyes with black food colour, so that two faces appear to be frowning and the others seem sleepy. Leave to dry before fitting the beaks which are folded diamond-shaped pieces of red and yellow paste.

The only parts not hardened before assembly are the birds' wings and tails which must be draped around the bodies and arranged differently for each bird. The champagne bottle is a piece of solid green paste, painted with black and gold food colour. Arrange the birds on the cake, adding the bottle, scroll and holly leaves.

1

2

1 To make the rings on the top of the cake, roll out some marzipan (almond paste) and paint it with food colour. Slice it into strips and roll them up tightly. Then trim the sides of the roll so that they are smooth. Slice a layer from the roll, lay it flat and roll it out until it is large enough to fit the top of the cake.
2 Making a robin: the pieces of paste, showing the stages in modelling the bird and marking its features, as described above.

Handy Hint

If you always opt for a 'snow scene', why not try this cake instead. It is simply a different way to rough ice a cake. Although the finished cake may look complicated, it can be iced quickly and you can afford to spend extra time painting the faces.

CHRISTMAS BOOT

If, like the 'Old Woman who Lived in a Shoe' in the children's rhyme, you need a large Christmas cake, this one is entirely suitable. It is two cakes in fact, an oval one and a smaller round one which fits on one end to make the ankle and top of the boot.

HANDY HINT

This cake is an awkward shape to cover with paste, so if the paste starts to fold or split, work that area into one of the wrinkles or around the area at the back of the heel. Disguise cracks by indenting a series of regular thread-like lines around the problem area, to look like a row of stitching along a seam.

MAKING A CARPET BASE

A carpet base can be made for the boot by covering the cakeboard with coloured sugarpaste and impressing it with a basketweave rolling pin. A fringe may also be cut at each end of the carpet.

25 x 18cm (10 x 7 inch) oval fruit cake
15cm (6 inch) round cake
1.25kg (2½ lb) Sugarpaste, see page 8
variety of modelled figures and toys, see pages 18 – 22
red paste food colour
750g (1½ lb) Marzipan (almond paste), see page 8
60ml (2 fl oz/¼ cup) sherry, brandy or rum
250g (8 oz/1 cup) Royal Icing, see page 9
gold dragees (nonpareils)

EQUIPMENT

36 x 25cm (14 x 10 inch) cake board
palette knife
paintbrush

Prepare the boot by cutting and assembling the cakes as shown below. Colour 750g (1½ lb) sugarpaste red. Reserve a little white sugarpaste, then use the remainder to model the toys and figures.

Cover the cake with a layer of marzipan (almond paste). Before the paste hardens, brush with sherry, brandy or rum, except for the hollow on the smaller section. Cover the boot with the red sugarpaste, using your hands to smooth the paste around the bulges. Tuck the bottom edge of the paste underneath the cake so that it has a rounded appearance. Cut a 15cm (6 inch) circle out of the red paste in the hollow. Brush this area with alcohol and replace the red paste with a circle of white sugarpaste. Model a few holly berries from the remnants of red sugarpaste.

Use a palette knife to smooth a generous amount of royal icing around the top edge of the boot, then swirl it with a paintbrush into a bold pattern to represent the boot's fur lining. Leave this to dry. Add the figures and toys to the boot, with the holly berries and gold dragees (nonpareils).

The ankle of the boot is built up by fitting the 15cm (6 inch) round cake onto the end of the oval cake. Cut a cone-shaped hollow into the top of the round cake so that, when it has been iced, the toys and models will rest in it. Stick strips of marzipan to the cake with piping gel to create the wrinkles in the surface of the boot before applying the covering of marzipan.

MERRY CHRISTMAS CAKE

A strong design in bright and clear colours gives this bell-shaped cake a very festive feel. There are two forms of run-out used here: the design on the top is flooded directly onto the icing, while the trees and parcels arranged on the sides are flooded onto wax paper and attached to the cake later.

HANDY HINT

When working with light and dark colours, such as white and red, flood the light areas first and let them dry before applying the darker colour. So long as the set flooding is kept in a dry atmosphere, the white will not absorb any of the red from a neighbouring area.

25 x 23cm (10 x 9inch) flat bell-shaped cake
750g (1½ lb) Marzipan (almond paste), see page 8
1.25kg (2½ lb) Sugarpaste, see page 8
500g (1 lb/2 cups) Royal Icing, see page 9
red, blue, green, yellow, pink and skintone paste food colours
piping gel
3 holly leaves, see page 15

EQUIPMENT

36 x 33cm (14 x 13 inch) bell-shaped cake board
non-stick teflon-coated cloth or wax paper
nos. 1 and 0 piping tubes (tips)
piping bags
paintbrush
1 metre (40 inch) of 3mm (⅛ inch) wide red ribbon

Cover the cake with marzipan (almond paste) and sugarpaste. Cover the board with sugarpaste and set both aside to dry separately. Place the cake on the board. It is important to plan the order of applying the icing before you begin. As you trace the pattern, see page 25, and transfer it to the cake top, give some thought to the different parts of the design and work out which sections to fill in first. It is best to start with those parts of the design which appear to be the most distant. Then, if there is any overlap between the icing on different sections, those parts which appear nearer overlap those further away. For the little girl in this picture, the arm and the stocking are closest, so they should be flooded after the main part of her gown. Follow the instructions on flooding on page 14. Start with the white sections, even if they do appear to be closer, or there is a risk of the red colour bleeding into the white.

The same principal applies when flooding the side pieces, which are made on a non-stick mat, so complete the tubs before you fill in the Christmas trees. Allow at least 24 hours for the designs to dry before releasing them and attaching them to the cake with royal icing.

The parcels on the stocking are flooded separately and attached with a little royal icing when completely dry. The toe and heel areas of the stocking are overpiped using a no. 1 piping tube (tip) and the buttons on the front of the gown are added using the same tube (tip). A little stiff white royal icing is added to the edges of the hat and gown, and roughened with a paintbrush. Paint the details of the hair and face outline using skintone food colour.

Pipe the greeting on the cake using a no. 1 piping tube (tip) and red royal icing of normal piping consistency. Finish the cake with a narrow ribbon around the bottom edge, attached with piping gel. Attach the three holly leaves on the top of the stocking after the parcels have been positioned and secure them with a dot of royal icing.

Merry Christmas

BURGUNDY CAKE

Elegant and classical best describe this burgundy-coloured Christmas celebration cake, with three slender candles which lend a touch of romance to the design.

20cm (8 inch) square cake
750 g (1½ lb) Marzipan (almond paste), see page 8
1kg (2 lb) Sugarpaste, see page 8, coloured deep pink
burgundy paste food colour
125g (4 oz/½ cup) Royal Icing, see page 9
gold dragees (nonpareils)

EQUIPMENT

28 cm (11 inch) square thin cake board
no. 9 holly leaf crimper
star and cone modelling tools
confectioners' glaze
set of holly leaf cutters
rose leave veiners
3 x 13 cm (5 inch) slim pink candles
piping bags
nos. 1 shell and 43 piping tubes (tips)
1.5 metres (1¾ yd) burgundy tartan ribbon

Cover a fruit cake with marzipan (almond paste) and leave to dry for 1 – 2 days. Then cover the cake with pink sugarpaste. Before the sugarpaste begins to harden, make a paper template to fit around the sides of the cake. Fold the template into eight and cut it into a curve across the top. Unfold the paper, then pin this scallop pattern around the cake and use it as a guide to position the holly leaf design. Impress the design in the soft paste using a crimper or a holly cutter. Use a star modelling tool to impress the central vein on each leaf and use the cone modelling tool to indent the holly berries between each leaf.

The leaves, parcels and the larger balls on the top of the cake are made from the scraps of paste left after covering the cake. Cut six 2.5cm (1 inch) cubes for the pink parcels, then colour the remaining paste deep burgundy. Roll four balls of paste the same size as the parcels and leave these to dry, then dip them in confectioners' glaze.

Make 16 large, 15 medium and 14 small holly leaves, see page 15. Mark their veins with rose leaf veiners and leave to dry. Paint the leaves with two layers of confectioners' glaze so that they have a high gloss.

Dampen the back of a piece of soft sugarpaste about the size of a golf ball and place it on the centre of the cake, flatten it slightly and insert the three candles into it. Using a no. 1 piping tube (tip) and burgundy royal icing, pipe the ribbons around the parcels and attach these and the glazed balls to the cake with royal icing. Push the tips of the holly leaves into the central ball of paste and leave to set.

Add a few gold dragees (nonpareils) to give the centrepiece extra sparkle. Finish the cake with a shell border around the base and a bow of ribbon.

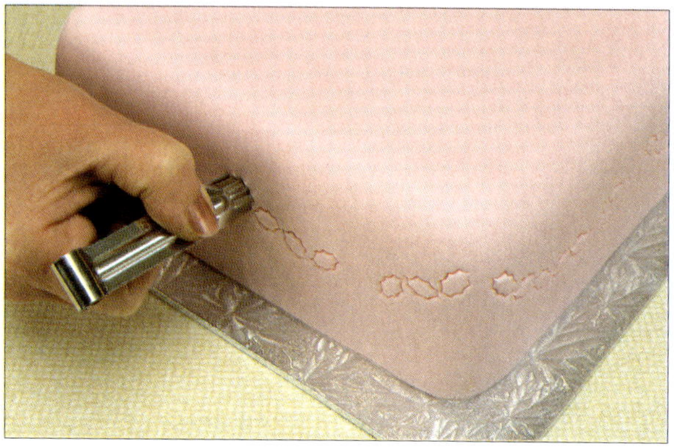

Embossing with crimping tools is a basic and simple technique for marking patterns. As well as this holly shape there are hearts, diamonds and scallops and they are available in widths from 1 – 3.5cm (½-1½ inch). Use them to press the pattern into soft sugarpaste coating.

HOLLY CAKE

Simplicity is the keynote of this sugarpaste-decorated cake which can be assembled in a matter of minutes once the pastillage pieces are dry. If preferred, royal icing may be used for the coating.

23cm (9 inch) round cake
1kg (2 lb) Marzipan (almond paste), see page 8
1.75kg (3½ lb) Sugarpaste, see page 8
185g (6 oz) Pastillage, see page 10
dark green and red paste food colour
red, yellow and blue dusting powders
125g (4oz/½ cup) Royal Icing, see page 9
cornflour (cornstarch)

EQUIPMENT

33cm (13 inch) round cake board
no. 5 piping tube (tip)
1 metre (40 inch) of 1cm (½ inch) wide scarlet ribbon for board edging
12cm (4½ inch) long holly leaf cutter
clear corrugated P.V.C. sheeting
confectioners' glaze (optional)

Cover the cake with marzipan (almond paste) and set aside for 1 – 2 days. Coat the cake board with sugarpaste the day before covering the cake.

Colour about 155g (5 oz) of the pastillage dark green, make sure that it is mixed by thoroughly kneading for several minutes. Store this paste in a plastic bag and cut off just enough to make about two or three leaves at a time. Roll out the paste to a thickness of about 2mm (⅛ inch), which is perfect for most pastillage that is to be used flat or moulded into simple curves. Curve the leaves as shown below. Cut out 20 leaves: although you will only use about 15 on the cake it is wise to make a few extra in case of breakages. Leave in a dry, warm place for 24 hours.

The flame is made from white pastillage: using the same holly cutter, cut two leaves, then cut a 2 mm (⅛ inch) slot from the base up the centre of the leaf. This slot should be 5cm (2 inch) long and it should end about midway along the length of the leaf. Take the second leaf and cut a similar slot, this time cutting from the tip down to the middle of the leaf. Let the leaves dry flat for 24 hours, then colour them with red and yellow dusting powder to represent a flame as shown below. Dust just a touch of blue into the base of the flame. Slot the two leaves together.

Make the candle from a thick sausage of white sugarpaste, about 5cm (2 inch) high by 7.5cm (3 inch) wide. Wrap a layer of red sugarpaste around the outside. While the paste is soft, mould one end to a slight peak on one side. Form a depression in the centre. Indent a lip into one side of the candle for the wax to run out. Push the flame into the centre while the paste is soft.

Pipe a row of small shells around the base of the cake. When the holly leaves are dry, clean the edges with a sharp craft knife or emery board. Stick them to the cake using a dab of icing behind each one. Make holly berries by rolling small balls of red sugarpaste: you can make them shine by dipping them in confectioners' glaze and letting them dry. Use a little royal icing to stick three berries at the base of each leaf.

If you have any royal icing, run some down the candle to make the pool of wax, otherwise use soft sugarpaste and mould it to shape. Finally, glue the scarlet ribbon around the edge of the board.

1

2

1 Lightly dust the corrugated sheeting with cornflour. Lay the leaves along the ridges as soon as they are cut. Make sure that all the leaves take on the same curve.
2 Apply dusting powder to hardened paste using a fairly large brush. Stipple the colour on, working from the outside edge into the middle of the flower or leaf. Always work on a piece of kitchen roll or tissue as it is easier to clean up.

HANDY HINTS

- *So that its easier to line up all the holly leaves when they are set out to dry, draw a guide line along the underside of the plastic sheet using a felt-tipped pen. The best way to cut corrugated PVC sheeting at home, is by using a pair of strong kitchen scissors.*
- *Use dark brown and a touch of red to shade the green pastillage to a really dark green colour. Colours lighten as the paste dries out.*
- *It is vital that the slots in the leaves are cut to exactly the midpoint along the length of the leaf. If they do not meet the leaves will not slot together to form the candle shape.*

TEMPLATES

FOR SPECIAL DESIGNS

Bygone Days,
see page 76

The Arrangement of Toys in The Window

Season's Greetings,
see page 52

JOIN

Dove of Peace, see page 62

Angels and Lambs, see page 60

Season's Greetings, see page 52

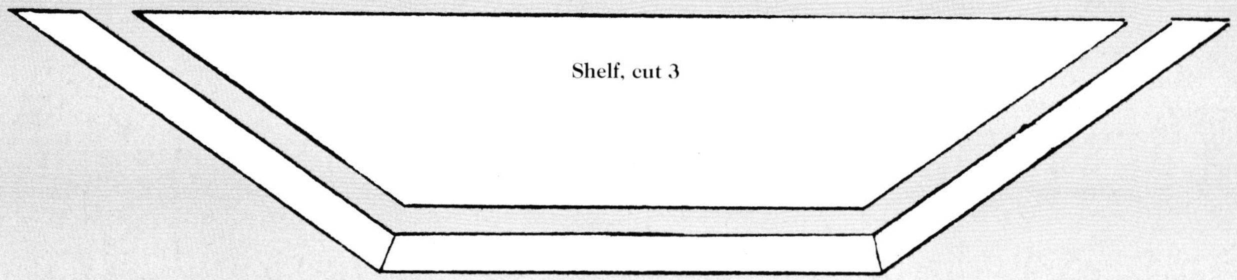

Lintel and Window Ledge, cut 2

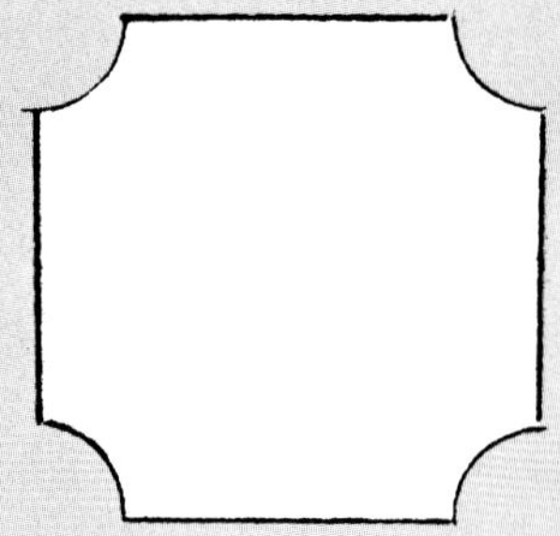

Fascia

Door Panel

Bygone Days, see page 76

Frame

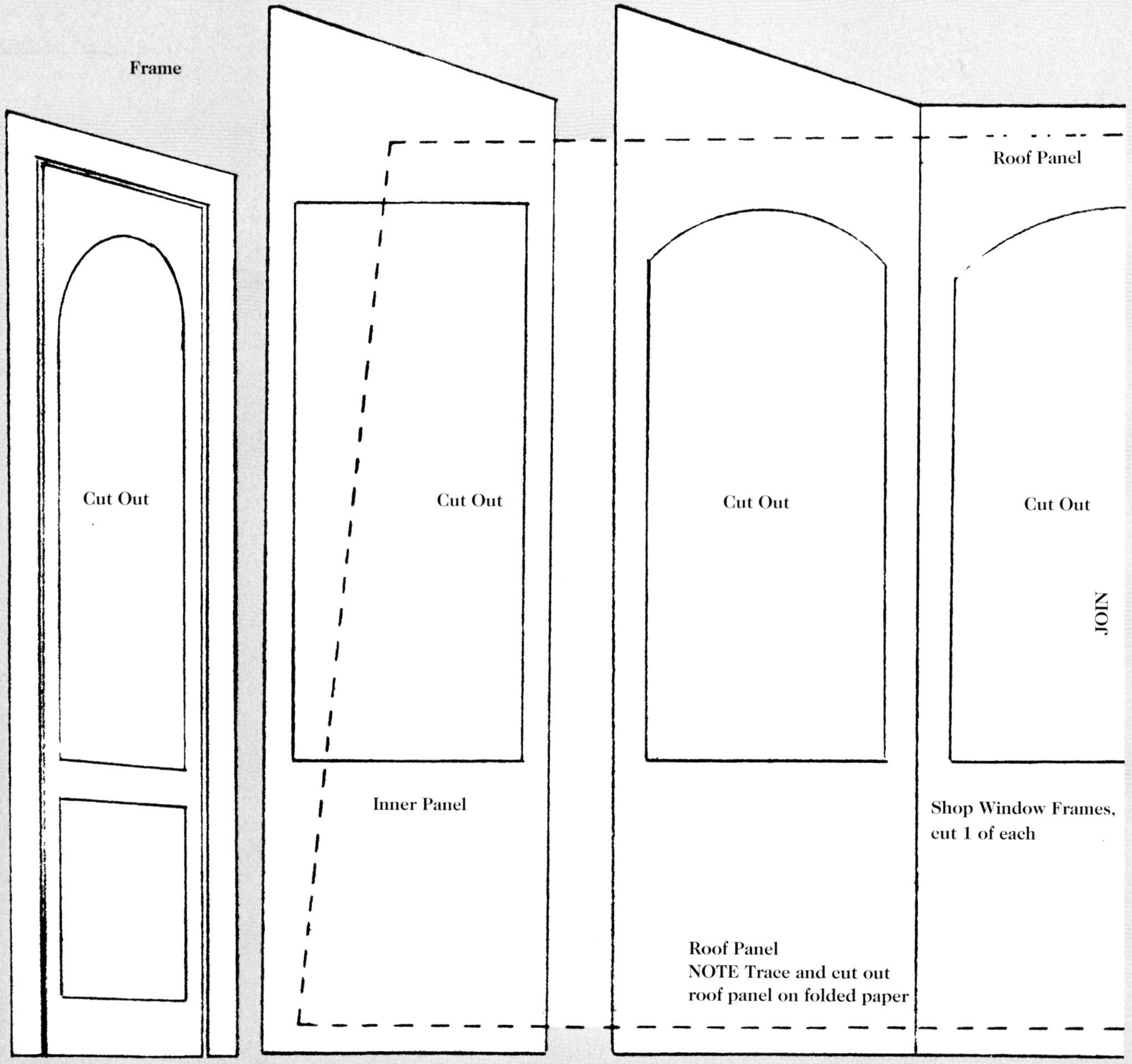

Setting Up The Cake
Diagram to show how the cake is set up on two boards before roof or window are fitted

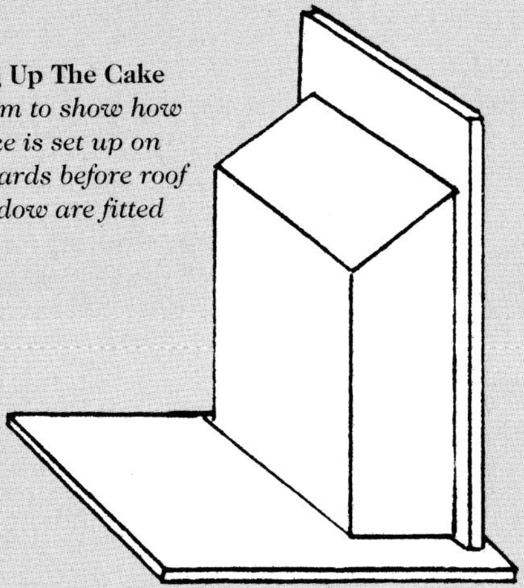

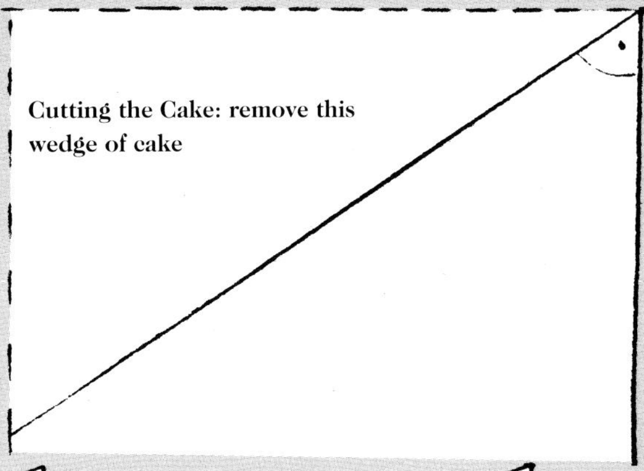

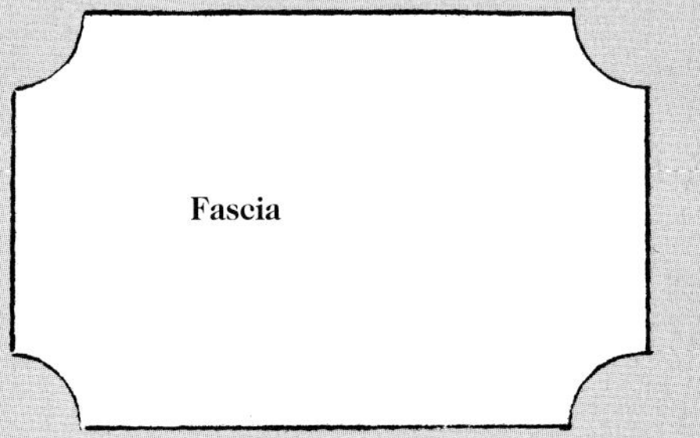

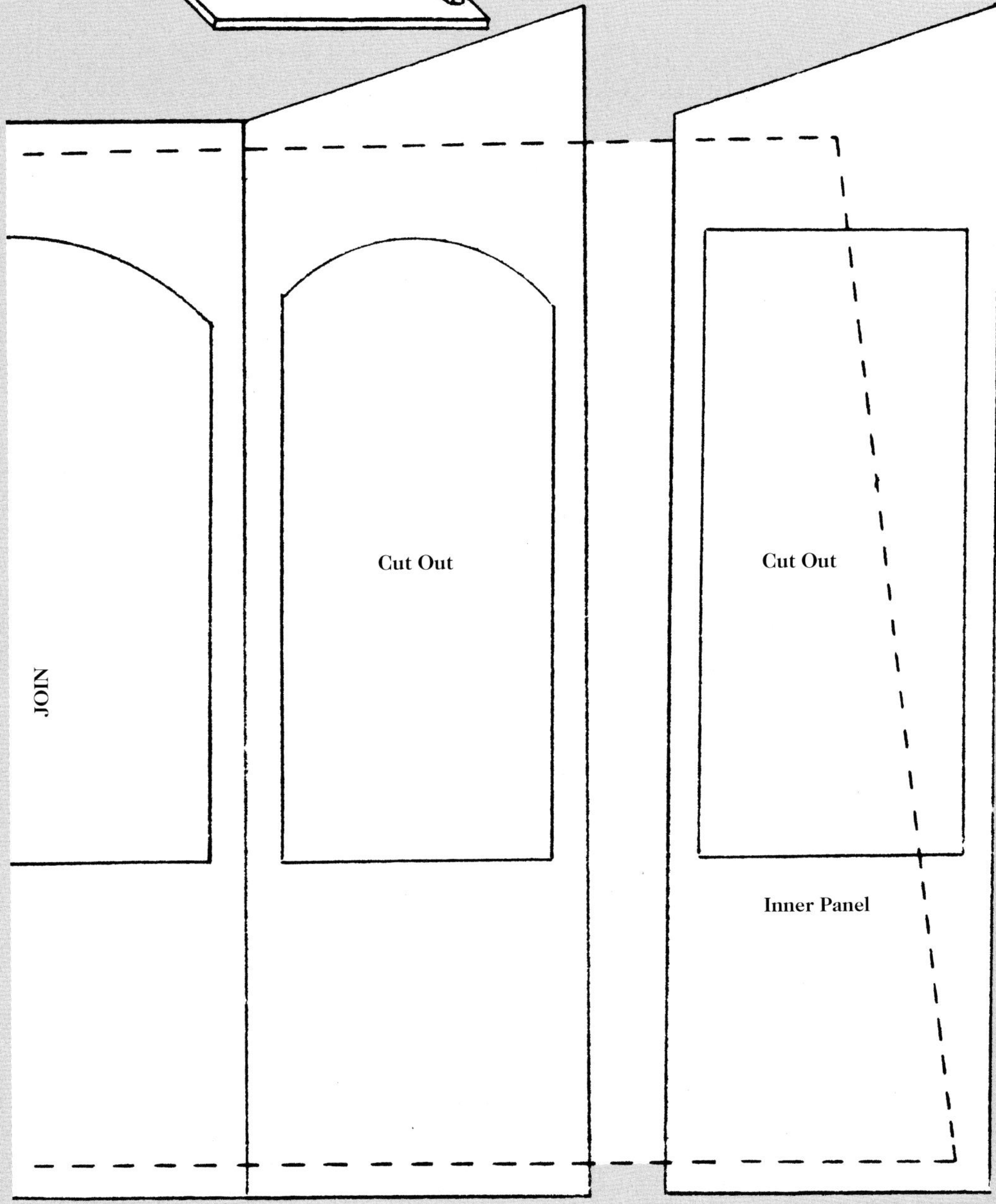

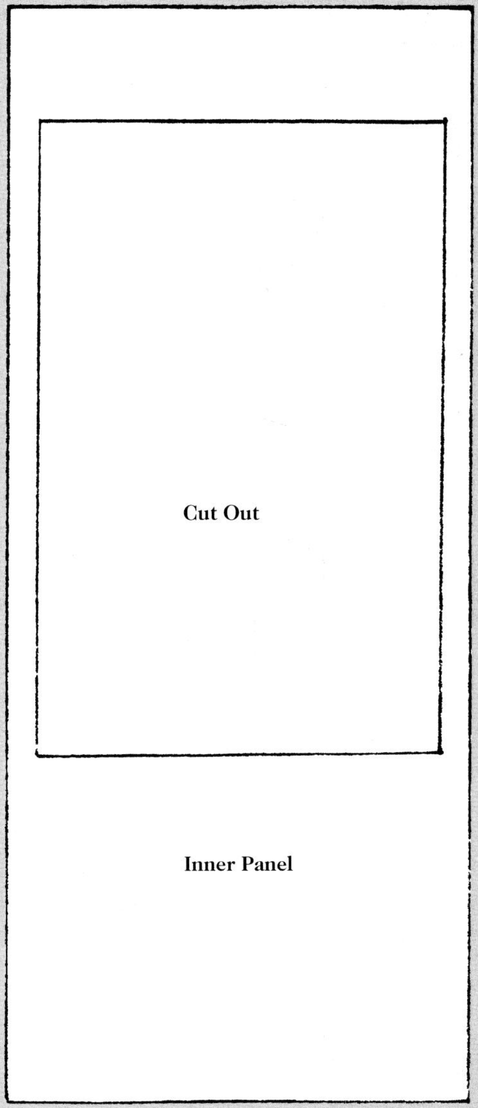

SEASON'S GREETINGS

Where I grew up, Christmas always took place in the heat of the summer, so I have only once seen snow on Christmas day. It was this thought that prompted me to decorate a cake which reminds me of the fact that the first Christmas took place in a town far away from holly, ivy and jolly looking robins.

23cm (9 inch) round cake
1kg (2 lb) Marzipan (almond paste), see page 8
1.5kg (3 lb) Royal Icing, see page 9
cornflower blue paste food colour
cornflower blue and silver snowflake dusting powders

EQUIPMENT

30cm (12 inch) round cake board
nos. 7 shell, 42 rope, 52 leaf and 3, 2, and 1.5 writing tubes (tips)
flat watercolour paintbrush
large and small piping bags
fine paintbrush
1 metre (40 inch) blue brocade ribbon
1 metre (40 inch) of 1 cm (½ inch) wide silver paper banding

Cut out the silhouette pattern on page 49 using cartridge paper or smooth-surfaced card.

Cover the cake with marzipan (almond paste) and leave to dry for 3 – 4 days. Then coat the cake with at least three coats of royal icing. Lay the stencil pattern on the cake. Mask the stencil with a piece of heavy plastic, such as a floppy mat, to prevent any stray colour from finding its way under the card. Mix cornflower blue colour with an equal proportion of silver snowflake and stipple it over the stencil with a flat watercolour brush. Work on a small section at a time starting from the centre of the cake and moving out towards the edge. It is a good idea also to mask the cake board if you have already coated it with royal icing

Using a large bag and a no. 7 star piping tube (tip), pipe 'C' and 'S' scrolls around the edge and base of the cake. Overpipe the scrolls, first using a no. 42 rope piping tube (tip), then a no. 3 writing tube (tip). Overpipe with another row of white icing using a no. 2 piping tube (tip). Finish with blue icing, piped using a no. 1.5 piping tube (tip). It is most important when piping scrolls, to ensure that the icing is well beaten and it should have lost its shiny look.

Use a no. 3 piping tube (tip) and white icing to pipe the seasonal message onto the cake. Overpipe using a no. 2 piping tube (tip) and white icing, then use a no. 1.5 piping tube (tip) and blue icing, to complete the overpiping.

Trim the cake with a bold-patterned ribbon in colours which complement the shades used for the icing decoration.

STENCILLING TIPS

- *If you want to re-use a card stencil, paint it with a mixture of equal parts of linseed oil and turpentine, then let it dry thoroughly for several days before using it for the first time. Do not use it until it is completely dry.*
- *A very delicate stencil is easier to cut from plain writing paper than from card. You can stiffen the cut-out by coating it with spray fabric starch, then ironing it as though it is a piece of fabric.*

1

2

1 When dusting around a stencil it is vital to keep the card close to the surface to prevent colour from getting under it. Stipple the colour carefully around the design. Move the floppy mat so that it is always close to the area where colour is being applied.
2 The finishing touch is to overpipe the pattern of blue icing on the scrolls and lettering. Use a no. 1.5 piping tube (tip) and follow the pattern already iced on the base and top edge of the cake.

Seasons Greetings

FATHER CHRISTMAS IN BED

Santa has completed his work for the year and, despite the size of his bed, he looks utterly relaxed. His head and feet are made from sugarpaste but his body and pillow are pieces of cake.

Patchwork Quilt

When making the patchwork quilt bedcover, make the patches from a mixture of one-quarter pastillage to three-quarters sugarpaste. Then they will be slightly harder than the sugarpaste base and will sink into it under the weight of a rolling pin without stretching too much. Keep the base and the patches covered until you are ready to stick them together. Work quickly and arrange the cover on the bed as soon as it is completed.

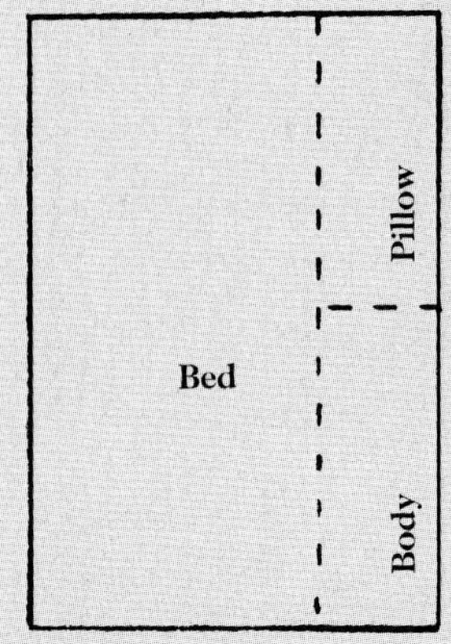

750g (1½ lb) Pastillage, see page 10
red, yellow, skintone, dark brown, blue, green and pink paste food colours
2kg (4 lb) Sugarpaste, see page 8
25 x 18cm (10 x 7 inch) oblong cake
1kg (2 lb) Marzipan (almond paste), see page 8
250g (8 oz/1 cup) Royal Icing, see page 9

EQUIPMENT

36 x 25cm (14 x 10 inch) thin cake board
straight edge or ruler
garrett frill cutter
no. 13 closed scallop mini crimper
set of modelling tools
fine-pointed scissors
floppy mat
tracing wheel
nos. 1 writing and 43 rope piping tubes (tips)
large and small piping bags
small holly leaf cutter
small leaf veiner
confectioners' glaze
Gum Arabic Glue, see page 9

Colour 500g (1 lb) pastillage bright yellow and use to make the bed ends, using the pattern on page 56. Leave to dry overnight. Marble 500g (1 lb) brown sugarpaste with white or yellow streaks and use to cover the cake board. Indent parallel lines across the board with the edge of a ruler or straight edge, so that the result looks like wooden floorboards.

Cut the cake as shown in the diagram, left. Cover the larger piece with a layer of marzipan (almond paste), then a layer of white sugarpaste. Place this in position on the board, allowing enough room for the bed-ends and blanket.

Shape the remaining two portions of cake, one to make the pillow and the other for Santa's body, and cover them with marzipan. Cover the pillow with blue sugarpaste. Attach a frill and crimp the paste where it is attached to the pillow. Set the pillow and then the body in place on the bed. Pipe the decorative designs on the bed-ends using a no. 1 piping tube (tip) and set them against the bed with a little royal icing.

Knead 250g (8 oz) pastillage with the same quantity of sugarpaste and colour the paste skintone. Make the head from a 185 – 220g (6 – 8 oz) ball of this paste. Indent the eyes and mould a nose before placing the head on the pillow. Using the pattern as a guide, mould the hands, arms and feet. Place the feet over the end of the bed with the upper part of the legs resting on the pad of cake which represents Santa's body. Dress the tops of the arms with sleeves made from red sugarpaste, bend them into shape, then cover the arms with plastic wrap to stop them from drying.

Make the patchwork bedcover about 35 x 18cm (14 x 7 inch) in size. As soon as the patches are rolled into the blue icing, use a modelling tool or a needlework tracing wheel to indent the patches so that they look as though they are sewn in place. Drape the cover across the bed, so that the upper edge is arranged close to Santa's face. Place the arms in position, tucking the upper ends between the bedcover and the pillow.

Cut a 13cm (5 inch) circle of red sugarpaste, then cut it in half and form a cone from one portion for the night cap. Model a pair of slippers from red paste and arrange them in the positions shown. Make a Christmas cracker from a piece of leftover paste.

Finally, pipe stiff royal icing using a no. 43 piping tube (tip) around the face to create a bushy beard and moustache and brush it into swirls. This icing conceals the joins around the head and shoulders. To complete the cake, pipe icing around the sleeves and the night cap and add the pom-pom to the cap. Attach the holly leaves and berries to the end of the bed.

Slippers

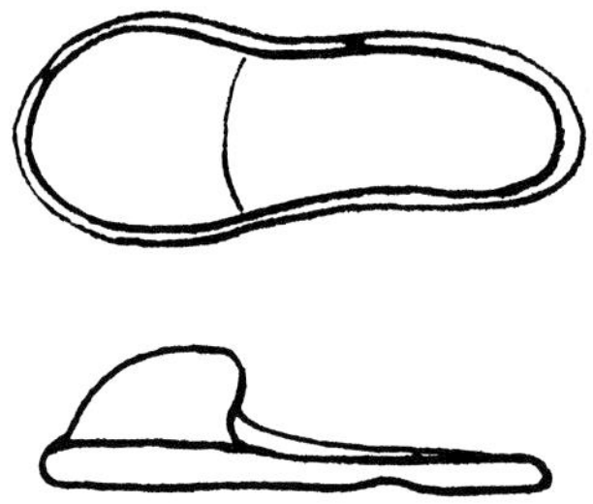

Christmas Cracker

CHRISTMAS BELL

This bell-shaped cake is a Christmas classic. With a triple row of frills and a top piece of poinsettias, winter roses and holly, it is sure to be a popular choice.

2kg (4 lb) Dolly Varden, tiffin or bell-shaped cake
750g (1½ lb) Marzipan (almond paste), see page 8
1.75kg (3½ lb) Sugarpaste, see page 8
60ml (2 fl oz) rum, brandy or sherry
500g (1 lb) Pastillage, see page 10
red, jade green, apple green and dark brown paste food colours
125g (4 oz/1/2 cup) Royal Icing, see page 9
moss green dusting powder
leaf green Sugartex

EQUIPMENT

30cm (12 inch) round gold cake board
2.5cm (1 inch) single scallop crimper
bell embosser • scriber
garrett frill cutter
cocktail stick (toothpick)
no. 1 writing tube (tip)
piping bag
flower pick • paintbrush
set of holly cutters • rose leaf veiners
medium all-in-one rose cutter
large rose calyx cutter
set of 4 poinsettia cutters
28 gauge green floristry wire
33 gauge white floristry wire
green floristry tape • set of modelling tools
fine-pointed scissors • confectioners' glaze
Gum Arabic Glue, see page 9

Cover the cake with marzipan (almond paste) and leave to set for 1 – 2 days. Cover the cake board with white sugarpaste and use a large scallop crimper to trim the edges of the paste while it is still soft. Emboss each scallop with a bell embosser.

Roll out 1kg (2 lb) sugarpaste into a 46cm (18 inch) circle. Brush the cake with rum, brandy or sherry and cover with the sugarpaste. Smooth the surface then set the cake on the board. Leave to dry.

Use a scriber to scratch a faint line of scallops around the base of the cake, to use as a guide for attaching the rows of frills. Knead 250g (8 oz) pastillage with an equal quantity of sugarpaste and divide the paste into three equal portions. Leave one part white, colour one piece red and the third piece green.

Roll out the red paste and then cut out a scalloped circle using the garrett frill cutter. Frill the paste, cut one side of the circle and open it out. Stick the frill to the cake with a little water. Continue attaching red frills around the cake. Then repeat the process with the green and white pastes. Using a no. 1 piping tube (tip) and red royal icing, pipe a row of three dots around the top of the white frill.

Insert a long cone-shaped flower pick into the top of the cake to house the stems of the wired flowers. The wires should never be in contact with the cake.

Divide the remaining pastillage into three: colour one portion deep red, another deep green, and leave the third portion white. Make one large red poinsettia with 18 – 20 petals, eight Christmas roses and about 25 – 30 holly leaves. Glaze the leaves before you begin to wire together the floral top piece.

1

2

1 Make the frill following the instructions on page 20.
2 Cut and open out the ring of paste. Dampen the cake at the position where the frill is to be attached, then press the top edge of the frill onto the cake. The upper edge of the frill may be embossed using a crimper or a modelling tool.

SUGARTEX

Sugartex is a granular, sugar-based coloured product used for creating the centres of flowers. Alternatively, caster sugar may be tinted with a little food colour.

MARKING THE SCALLOPS

Make a paper template to fit around the cake. Fold it into six and draw the scallop curve on the folded paper, then cut it out. Open out the paper and place it around the cake, holding it carefully in place as you mark the shape of each scallop.

MAKING THE FLOWER SPRAY

1 HOLLY LEAVES Wired leaves are made from pastillage which is deliberately left thicker at one edge than the other when rolled out. This allows room for the wire stalk to be pushed into the leaf. Vein the leaf on a plastic veiner. Then use a dogbone modelling tool to thin the edges and shape the leaf. Dip the leaves into the bowl containing confectioners' glaze to make them glossy, then hang them up to dry. To obtain a high gloss, dip them a second – or even a third – time, to build a thick glaze.

2 CHRISTMAS ROSES Roll out a piece of green pastillage leaving a conical point at the centre. Cut out a calyx by placing the cutter over the conical point and insert a hooked wire into the point. Leave to dry. Use the all-in-one cutter to stamp out the flower. Cup the petals by pressing them into a resilient foam pad using a modelling tool and soften their edges by rolling with the ball modelling tool. Stick the soft flower to the hard calyx with gum arabic glue and dry.

Dust the centre of the flower with moss green dusting powder, then pipe a small amount of royal icing into it. The bowl contains coloured powdered sugar: pour some into the bloom, then tip it out again. The small amount of sugar which remains represents stamens.

3 POINSETTIA Poinsettia flowers are made from individually wired petals of various sizes. Make them the same way as the holly leaves by leaving the stem end thick and inserting a fine white wire into the paste. Vein each petal and leave to set over foil, see page 15. Make about twenty petals of different sizes and about 6 – 7 green buds. Mould the buds onto wire, then snip their tops with fine-pointed scissors and tinge them with red paste food colour. The petals often straggle and appear to be arranged in no discernible pattern around the buds. All the wires are taped together into a thick strand at the back of the flower and bound with floristry tape.

4 ASSEMBLING THE FLOWER SPRAY Start by cutting the floristry tape in half lengthways. Bind together five or six holly leaves and then two Christmas roses, pulling the tape taut as you add each leaf or flower. Make four of these sprays.

The holly and Christmas roses are bound to the back of the poinsettia by securely taping each of the four holly sprays one at a time to the central stem. Do this until you have a large, and visually well-balanced, spray. Then insert the spray into the flower pick on the top of the cake.

MEXICAN HAT TECHNIQUE

Many flowers have a distinct calyx at the back of the bloom. The first stage in modelling a calyx is to roll out a piece of green pastillage leaving a conical point in the centre. This is called the 'mexican hat' technique because the shape is similar to that of a sombrero.

ANGELS AND LAMBS

Angels and lambs symbolise the spirit of Christmas on this Wedgwood blue cake, which is baked in a scalloped oval tin (pan). Pure white bas relief figures and a minimum of embellishment heighten the simplicity of the design.

Bas Relief Work

Bas relief work is easy if you plan the order in which the parts of the design must be assembled. Always work from the background to the foreground. The final pieces to be assembled are those which are appear closest to you.

1½ quantities Rich Fruit Cake, see page 7
1kg (2 lb) Marzipan (almond paste), see page 8
1.75kg (3½ lb) Sugarpaste, see page 8
250g (8 oz) Pastillage, see page 10
cornflower blue and violet paste food colours
silver snowflake dusting powder
250g (8 oz/1 cup) Royal Icing, see page 9

Equipment

25cm x 20cm (10 x 8 inch) scalloped oval tin (pan)
36 x 30cm (14 x 12 inch) scalloped oval cake board
nos. 43 rope, 0 and 1 writing tubes (tips)
piping bags
small holly leaf cutter
small leaf veiner
set of modelling tools
fine-pointed scissors
paintbrush
Gum Arabic Glue, see page 9
1 metre (40 inch) of 8mm (⅜ inch) wide blue ribbon

Preheat the oven to 140°C (275°F/Gas 1). Grease and line the tin (pan) with brown paper. Turn the cake mixture into the tin and bake it for 4 – 5 hours, or until a skewer inserted into the centre of the cake comes out clean. Leave the cake to cool in the tin. Cover the cake with marzipan (almond paste) and leave for 1 – 2 days.

Cover the board with 500g (1 lb) of the sugarpaste and mix 250g (8 oz) with the pastillage. Colour the remaining sugarpaste a deep Wedgwood blue by mixing a little violet colour with the cornflower blue. Cover the cake with this blue sugarpaste and let the icing harden for several days before attaching any of the bas relief design to it.

Use the pastillage and sugarpaste mixture for the bas relief figures. Lay a piece of oiled plastic over the pattern, see page 49. Make each part of the figure on the plastic following the order listed, right. Adjust the clothing so that it may be arranged in folds and tucks to fall naturally around the bodies. As each section is finished transfer it to the top of the cake. Try to complete and assemble all the design, except for the smaller angel's wings, before any of the pieces become too hard to fit snugly into place.

Cut out the wings from rolled paste using scissors and mark them with a fine modelling stick to resemble feathers. Support them in their upraised position on pads of foam sponge until they have set in place.

Cut eight holly leaves for the frieze on the side of the cake and make five bas relief lambs. Leave these to set. When they have hardened, pipe the wool on the lambs using royal icing and a no. 0 piping tube (tip). Leave to dry. Attach all the small decorations to the cake. Pipe the garlands with an interlocking teardrop shape design using a no. 1 piping tube (tip) and finish the base of the cake with a shell border, piped using a no. 43 piping tube (tip). Attach a band of dark blue ribbon to the edge of the cake board.

Order for Creating Bas Relief Design

Work from the most distant part of each figure and build up the design in the following order:

1 the larger angel's left arm and the lantern
2 the larger angel's head and lower wing
3 the lower limbs of both angels
4 the larger angel's gown
5 the larger angel's upper wing
6 the smaller angel's gown
7 the smaller angel's head and arm
8 the larger angel's right arm
9 the hair of both figures
10 the wings of the smaller angel
11 the lambs

1

2

3

1 Scratch the positions of the extremities of the bas relief figures onto the icing. These guidelines will ensure that the parts of the figures are correctly located as they are assembled. Then dust the beams of light radiating from the lantern.

2 Protect the pattern with a piece of lightly oiled polythene or plastic. The figures are constructed on this pattern. Only the parts which show need be modelled accurately, the limbs and remaining parts provide a foundation for the garments.

3 The larger angel's gown is thinly rolled pastillage, arranged in folds and tucked around her body and under the legs of the smaller angel. The nearer wing is resting against the back of the gown – it will not be attached until the more distant wing is positioned.

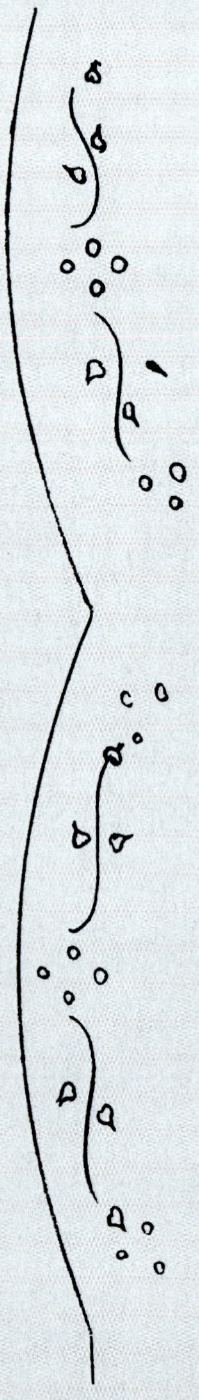

Side pattern

DOVE OF PEACE

A pure white dove bearing an olive branch, and pastillage bells embroidered with a simple pattern, combine peace and celebration – the true meaning of the Christmas message.

double quantity Rich Fruit Cake, see page 7
1.75kg (3½ lb) Sugarpaste, see page 8
jade paste food colour
1kg (2 lb) Marzipan (almond paste), see page 8
500g (1 lb) Pastillage, see page 10
500g (1 lb/2 cups) Royal Icing, see page 9

EQUIPMENT

25cm (10 inch) long fan-shaped tin (pan)
large 36 x 33cm (14 x 13 inch) fan-shaped cake board
no. 16, 1cm (½ inch) mini chevron crimper
scriber
fine-pointed scissors
set of mistletoe cutters
modelling stick
Gum Arabic Glue, see page 9
nos. 0 and 1 writing and 42 rope piping tubes (tips)
small piping bags
small leaf cutter
large bell mould
large carnation cutter
non-stick teflon-coated mat or wax paper
cranked palette knife
paintbrush
2 metres (2¼ yd) each of 3mm (⅛ inch) wide aqua and white ribbon

Preheat the oven to 140°C(275°F/Gas 1). Line the tin (pan) with brown paper. Turn the cake mixture into the tin and bake for 5 – 6 hours, until a skewer inserted into the centre of the cake comes out clean. Leave the cake to cool in the tin.

Reserve 250g (8 oz) white sugarpaste and colour the rest pale jade. Cover the cake with marzipan (almond paste), then cover with the pale jade sugarpaste. Deepen the colour of the leftover sugarpaste and use to cover the cake board. Crimp around the edge with the no. 16 mini chevron crimper. Put this aside to dry.

Use a scriber to scratch the outline of the dove pattern, see page 49, on the cake. Trace the pattern and cover it with a piece of lightly greased polythene.

Roll out about 60g (2 oz) pastillage and cut out the basic shape of the wings, then set these aside to dry. Mix half the pastillage with the white sugarpaste and mould the body and head of the dove by hand, comparing your work for accuracy occasionally by checking it against the template. Carefully build out the chest and head so that, while the underside of the bird is flat, the breast stands out from the template in a smooth semi-circular profile. If it becomes too rounded, simply cut away some of the paste with a pair of scissors.

Mistletoe cutters are the right shape for cutting the larger wing feathers. Use a small modelling stick to texture the paste, dragging it in parallel strokes down the length of each feather. Glue the tail feathers in position with gum arabic glue, then cover the lower wing with textured feathers.

Mould the body and head of the dove following the pattern. The pastillage base for the wings provides depth and texture. Let the wings harden, then stick feathers of textured, frilled paste onto them. The feathers of paste have yet to be added to the rear wing. Note the indented section on the dove's back - this will accommodate the end of the front wing.

Dove of Peace, continued from page 62

Pipe the upper stem of the olive branch, then attach the bird's body to the cake with gum arabic glue. Pipe the lower stem and stick small jade pastillage leaves along both stems.

Hide the join at the tail by covering the area with feathers cut with the small leaf cutter and ridged with the modelling stick. Cover the whole of the upper wing with feathers, working from the lower edge up to the leading edge which should be finished with one long feather. Attach the wing to the bird with royal icing and support it with a piece of foam sponge until it has set firmly in place.

Trace the side pattern on page 62 and scribe the design through the paper onto the side of the cake, then remove the paper. Pipe the shell border around the base of the cake using a no. 42 piping tube (tip) and white royal icing. Fill one small bag fitted with a no. 1 piping tube (tip) with jade icing and another bag fitted with the no. 0 piping tube (tip) with white icing. Begin piping the embroidery at the centre of the design. Pipe the forget-me-nots as a series of five tiny dots in white icing, and the leaves in jade in the shape of a teardrop on either side of a fine stem line.

Make eight loops in each colour ribbon and attach them into a small ball of sugarpaste stuck just behind the bells.

MOULDING BELLS

Use a plastic mould to form the half bells. Take a ball of pastillage about the size of a golf ball, roll it flat to a thickness of 1cm (½ inch). Dust the inside of the mould with cornflour (cornstarch) and press the rolled side of the paste into the mouth of the bell. Gradually work the paste into the dome of the bell, removing the paste from the mould from time to time. Use plenty of cornflour to help this process. Thin and smooth the flanged edge of the bell using the pad of the thumb. Cut off any excess paste. Turn the bell out of the mould and, while the paste is soft, trim the edge with a frill cutter. Then cut the bell in half. Put the two halves back into the bell mould and let them harden overnight before attempting to pipe the decoration onto the rim.

LACE AND DOVES

Use a no. 1 piping tube (tip) to pipe the delicate lacework in the form of bells and doves on a non-stick mat or wax paper. The lace must dry before removing each piece individually and attaching it to the cake with a tiny amount of royal icing. Never attempt to lift pieces of lace with tweezers: loosen them with the aid of a fine cranked palette knife and lift them between the fingers.

The doves are piped as shown, and following the diagram on the left. Stick the wings and tail into a teardrop of wet royal icing, with the tail at the pointed end. Pipe the head and beak and leave to set, then attach the dove to the cake with a dot of royal icing.

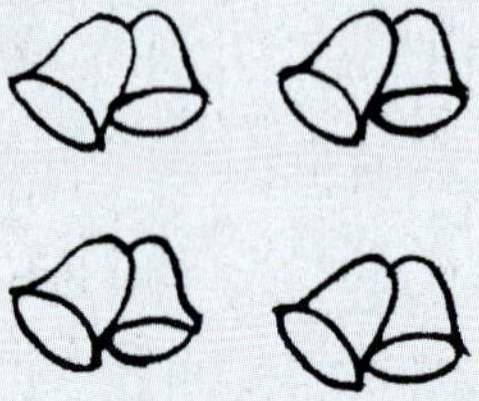

Lace Bells

Piped Doves

CHRISTMAS SNOWFLAKE

The rich red coating on this cake makes a perfect backdrop for white filigree snowflakes. Although they look extremely fragile, I have found the snowflakes to be surprisingly robust once they are attached to the cake.

20cm (8 inch) hexagonal cake
750g (1½ lb) Marzipan (almond paste), see page 8
1kg (2 lb) Sugarpaste, see page 8
extra-strong red paste food colour
500g (1 lb/2 cups) Royal Icing, see page 9

EQUIPMENT

30cm (12 inch) hexagonal cake board
nos. 0, 1 and 1.5 writing and 42 star piping tubes (tips)
small piping bags
teflon-coated non-stick mat or wax paper
1 metre (40 inch) of 1cm (½ inch) wide silver paper banding
1 metre (40 inch) of 5mm (¼ inch) wide red feather-edge ribbon
blocks of polystyrene or foam sponge

Cover the cake board with 250g (8 oz) white sugarpaste. Colour the remaining sugarpaste red. Cover the cake with marzipan and leave for 1 – 2 days, then cover it with red sugarpaste. Trim the edge of the cake board with silver banding and narrow red ribbon. Pipe a row of stars around the base of the cake using a no. 42 piping tube (tip).

The quality of the icing for the snowflakes is very critical, so take extra care with its preparation. Make sure the sugar is finely sifted. You can add a little extra albumen powder to the mixture when you make it up, or even add a pinch of gum arabic to the prepared icing to make it stronger. A trick which expert bakers used to employ, was to make the icing with egg whites which had been left standing, uncovered, for several days. This allowed some of their water content to evaporate causing the albumen to become concentrated and making a tougher icing.

You will need to pipe six small snowflakes to decorate the sides of the cake and one large one for the top decoration. In addition, you will need four half snowflakes (also made from the large pattern) to complete the top piece. It is also wise to make extra to allow for breakages!

Trace the patterns onto separate pieces of paper and place them on a flat board. Then cut a piece of non-stick mat or wax paper and tape it over the first of the patterns, allowing the pattern to be slid out easily. You can then remove the pattern and insert it beneath more pieces of non-stick material in order to pipe all the filigree snowflakes.

To maximize the strength of these extremely delicate filigree pieces, use a no. 1.5 piping tube (tip) for the straight lines, a no. 1 piping tube (tip) for the outline and a no. 0 piping tube (tip) for the dots, mini snowflakes and other embellishments on the basic structure.

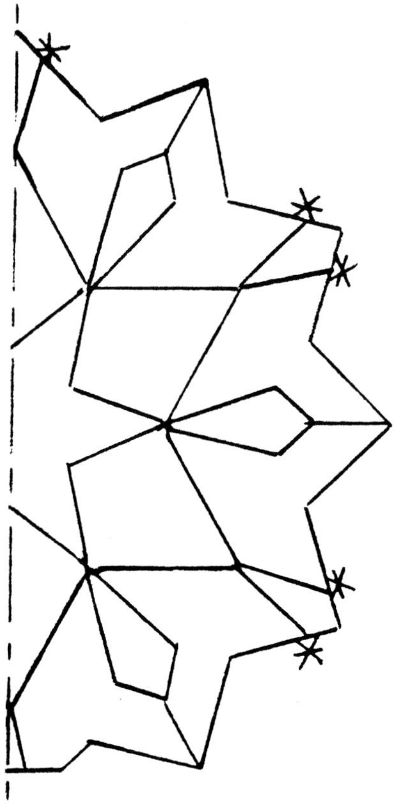

Large Snowflake for Top Piece

NOTE Trace the patterns on folded paper, then trace the shape again onto the underneath of the folded paper. Unfold the paper to show the complete snowflake.

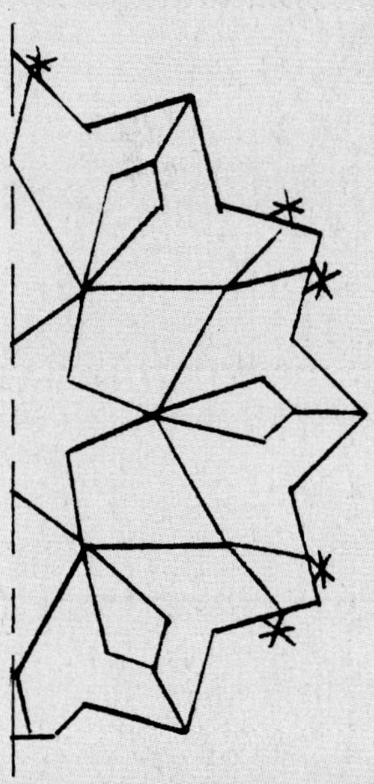

Small Snowflake for Cake Side

HANDY HINTS

- *Part of the snowflake pattern could be flooded. It will take a lot longer to dry and the edge of the star will need to be reinforced with a second line of piping to support the extra weight of icing.*
- *When piping the half snowflakes do not pipe a solid line across the centre star, or the snowflake will lose it's see-through appearance.*

ALIGNING THE TOP PIECE

So that the top piece looks the same from every angle, position the snowflake pieces in such a way that they line up with the six corners of the cake.

PIPING THE SNOWFLAKE

1 Pipe the snowflake onto a non-stick mat or wax paper. Make sure that the icing is in perfect condition by beating it just before filling the piping bag. The order in which the snowflake is piped is shown here: start with the centre star and its dots which form three-point lace. When piping the snowflake, it is best to pipe only one example on each piece of non-stick mat.

2 Delicate piped items can only be removed without breakage if the mat or paper is peeled away from the item, not the other way around. Slide the mat to the edge of the board and draw it downwards, keeping it taut, until the piped item is released. Then turn the mat around and repeat the action to release the remaining side of the piping.

ASSEMBLING THE TOP PIECE

1 Securing the first piece of the snowflake to the cake is a balancing act! First scratch a centre line on the cake surface. Have polystyrene or foam pads ready to support the star as soon as you stand it in position. Make sure your hands are perfectly dry before you start. Dust them with cornflour (cornstarch) or talcum powder, otherwise you may dissolve the icing as you handle it. Pipe a fine line of royal icing onto the cake following the scratched centre line and gently rest the edge of the snowflake in it. Do not try to lift the snowflake with a palette knife or tweezers, simply pick it up with your fingers and move it into position. Do not squeeze your fingers together. Place a second support in front of the snowflake while you release the side pieces from their non-stick mats.

2 Each additional piece of the snowflake must be carefully lifted and attached with a minute spot of royal icing. Although the structure is very delicate, once the first piece has set, it is not as difficult as it looks to join the other parts to the centrepiece. As soon as you have the second and third pieces in position, you can remove the supports and stick the final two sections in place. The most important thing is to avoid jogging the cake with a sudden movement. Once the top piece is complete, rest the smaller snowflakes against the cake sides, attaching each one with just a few spots of royal icing.

STORING THE CAKE

If you intend to store the cake for a week or longer, keep it in a dry, draught-free cupboard, where it will not be affected by sudden changes in temperature or humidity.

REINDEER AND SLEIGH

I first made this cake for my own children when they were very small. I think its popularity owed something to the fact that the sleigh was re-filled with little sweets every morning.

2.25kg (4½ lb) Sugarpaste, see page 8
30cm (12 inch) large oval cake
1kg (2 lb) Marzipan (almond paste), page 8
red, cornflower blue, ice blue, brown, black, green, pink and yellow paste food colours
750g (1½ lb/3 cups) Royal Icing, see page 9

EQUIPMENT

41cm (16 inch) oval cake board
no. 33 maxi 4cm (1½ inch) scallop crimper
nos. 1 and 1.5 writing and 42 rope piping tubes (tips)
large and small piping bags
teflon-coated non-stick mat or wax paper
nos. 1 and 3 sable paintbrushes
Gum Arabic Glue, see page 9

Allow 24 hours for the run-outs of the reindeer, Santa and the sleigh to dry before moving them in order to finish the backs. If time is short, begin by making these pieces before you cover the cake. Follow the instructions on page 70.

Cover the cake board with a large piece of white sugarpaste, so that there is an overlap all around the edge. Trim the edge with a no 33 maxi 4cm (1½ inch) scallop crimper to create a fluted design. Set aside to dry. Coat the cake with marzipan (almond paste) and leave for 1 – 2 days. Then coat with marbled sugarpaste, see below right. Do not be tempted to make the blue for the sky too dark as it overwhelms the cake design.

Once the cake is covered and on the board, trace the patterns on page 70 and transfer the design of the buildings and their roofs to the side of the cake. Use small pieces of rolled-out paste to make the walls, doors and windows and attach them by moistening the back of each piece with water. Impress patterns to simulate brickwork and other architectural details before you position the pieces.

Any scraps of coloured paste will be suitable for the roofs. Cut them and secure them above the walls. They do not need to be very accurate. This is a fantasy cake, so set your imagination free and make towers, spires, turrets, steeples, castle battlements and any other features which seem appropriate.

Roll out and cut a semi-circular pad of sugarpaste. Place this on the cake and cover it with a generous quantity of royal icing swirled into a pattern to look like fluffy clouds, see page 71. Before the icing hardens, attach the reindeer, sleigh and Santa Claus. As a finishing touch, use a no. 15 piping tube (tip) to pipe a harness from the animals to the sleigh with strands of royal icing. Fill the sleigh with presents or sweets.

1 The marbled effect on this cake is achieved by partly blending pieces of white and blue sugarpaste. Colour some of the paste blue, then add streaks of blue food colour to small amounts of white icing. Knead all the pieces together to combine them but do not knead the paste too much. Roll out the paste in the usual way.

2 Embellish the rooftops by covering them with royal icing snow. Apply it with an icing tube and work it into place with a fine paintbrush. If there is any icing left, use it to texture the sugarpaste covering the board.

HANDY HINT

Remember to flood the areas in white on Santa Claus and let them dry before adding the red. The white flooding may then be covered with rough royal icing to simulate fur when the figure is finished without any risk of the red colour bleeding into the white.

REINDEER AND SLEIGH TOP PIECE

OUTLINING AND FIRST FLOODING

Trace the patterns for the reindeer, sleigh and Santa, see page 68 and below, and cover them with a semi-transparent non-stick teflon-coated mat or wax paper. You will need nine reindeer, one Santa Claus and the five parts that make up the sleigh; however, make a few extras to allow for breakages.

The outlines, including the antlers of the reindeer, are piped using a no. 1 piping tube (tip) and royal icing in the appropriate colours. Then they are filled in with flooding icing and allowed to dry completely in a warm place for 24 hours.

DOUBLE FLOODING: FLOODING THE REVERSE OF THE FIGURES

Remove the run-outs and turn them over. Short pegs of floristry wire are attached with more royal icing as shown here. The large beads of icing on the back of the figures have been added because icing contracts as it dries out, therefore, without this extra material, the reindeer would appear to have concave bodies.

Fill in the backs of the figures with a coating of icing. There is no need to re-pipe the outlines around the reindeer, apart from on their antlers. Note that the back of Santa Claus is different from the front, so first pipe the outline for the back of his head and his sack, then flood these with the appropriate colours. When dry, use a no. 42 piping tube (tip) to pipe the fur around the bottom of his coat, the tops of his boots and the ends of his gloves.

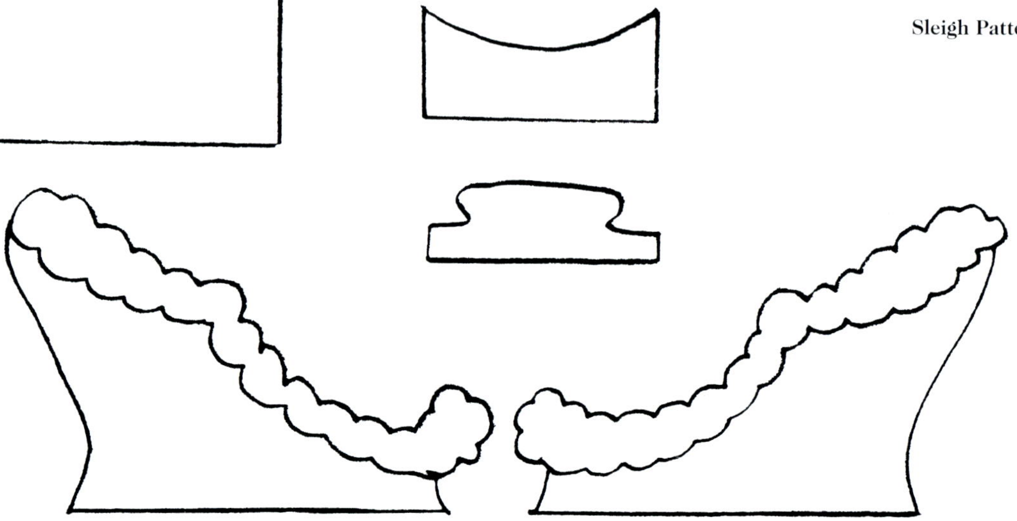

Sleigh Patterns

Adding Final Details of Decoration

Stick the sleigh together with red royal icing and pipe the details of the saddles and harnesses on both sides of the reindeer using red and green icing. Turn Santa Claus onto his back, then paint his face. Use a no. 42 piping tube (tip) to pipe the remaining fur on to his costume, his beard and hair.

Sugar lumps make delightful parcels when decorated with piped ribbons and bows.

Assembling the Decoration

It is not safe to stick wire into the cake itself when you position the figures, so roll out and cut a removable crescent-shaped pad of sugarpaste measuring about 1cm (½ inch) thick, and lay it on the cake. Cover the pad with a generous layer of rough royal icing, swirled to look like clouds, and set all the animals and figures into it. The pad, icing and top piece may be assembled separately, as here. It must be allowed to harden for at least 24 hours before transferring it to the top of the cake.

Pattern for Cake Side
Note This must be increased in size by 200% on a photocopier

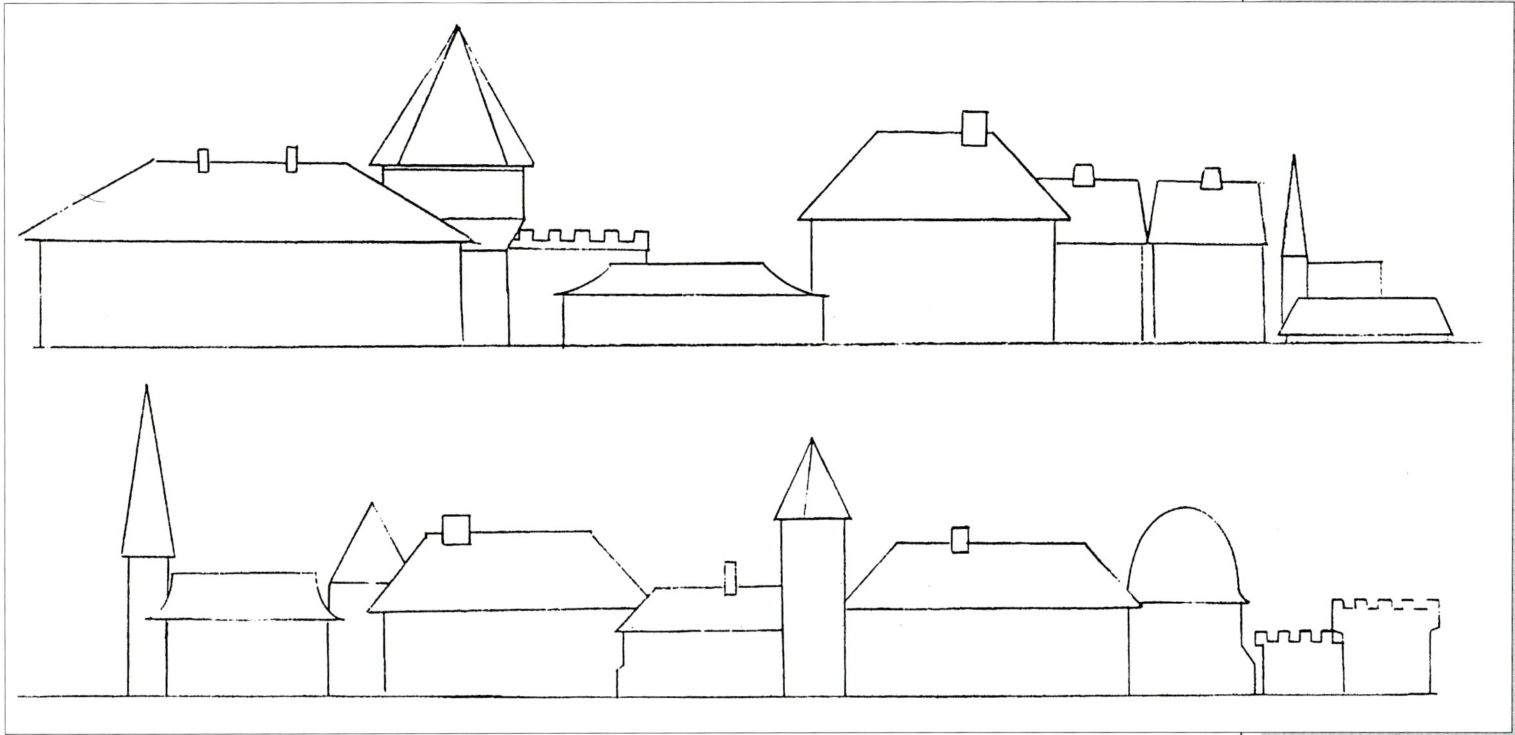

Side Design

NATIVITY SCENE

The nativity figures on my neighbour's mantelpiece inspired me to design this cake. The whole cake has been created in tones of cream and brown, highlighted with gold.

2.65kg (5¼ lb) Sugarpaste, see page 8
ivory, chestnut, skintone, dark brown, cream, red and black paste food colours
1kg (2 lb) Marzipan (almond paste), see page 8
30 x 23cm (12 x 9 inch) oblong octagon cake
125g (4 oz/½ cup) Royal Icing, see page 9
625g (1¼ lb) Pastillage, see page 10
non-stick baking spray
skintone dusting powder
gold food paint

EQUIPMENT

38 x 28cm (15 x 11 inch) oblong octagon thin cake board
no. 14 double scallop mini crimper
nos. 6 star and 1.5 writing piping tubes (tips)
piping bags
people moulds
cranked palette knife
Gum Arabic Glue, see page 9
set of modelling tools
scriber
fine-pointed scissors
no. 00 fine sable paintbrush
nos. 1 and 3 paintbrushes

Colour 2kg (4 lb) sugarpaste ivory, then colour 500g (1 lb) of this very dark brown. Leave the paste well wrapped for a few hours for the colour to develop and then use it to cover the cake board. Crimp around the edge and set aside to dry.

Cover the cake with marzipan (almond paste) and leave for 1 – 2 days. Then cover it with the remaining ivory sugarpaste and position it on the cake board. Finish by using a no. 6 star piping tube (tip) to pipe a shell border of brown royal icing around the base. Leave the cake to dry for a day or two while making the figures.

Knead the remaining white sugarpaste and the pastillage together. Set aside 125g (4 oz) of this white paste. Colour 375g (12 oz) skintone, 250g (8 oz) cream and 125g (4 oz) portions each of dark brown, light brown, chestnut and a red-brown.

The three kings, shepherds and angels are bas relief figures moulded in a similar manner to the angel on page 61. The patterns for the side design are shown on the left and on the following pages, to page 75

Side Design

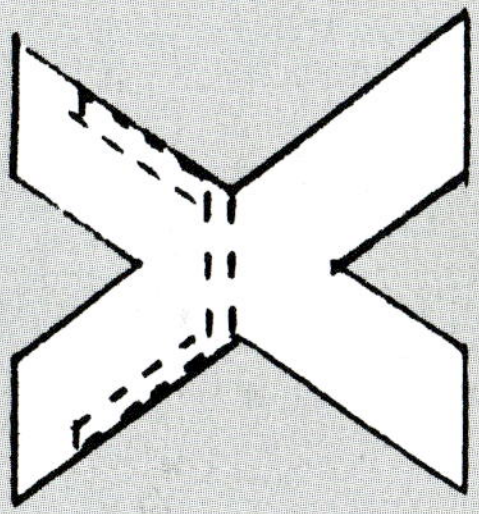

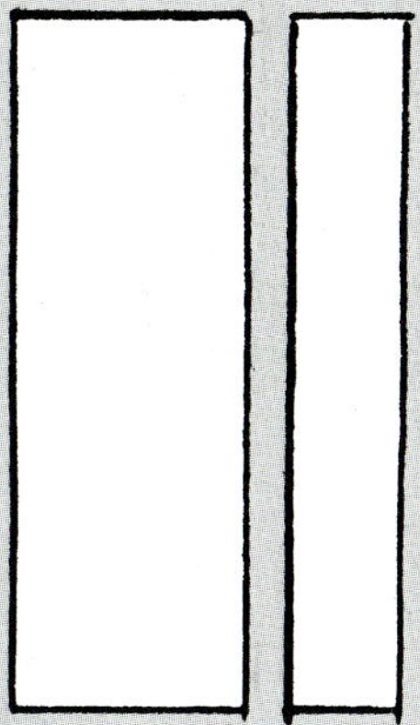

cut 2

Crib

MODELLING THE FIGURES

The free-standing figures are made on solid bases so that they will support themselves without having to use wire or cocktail sticks (toothpicks) to hold them together.

Grease the man's torso mould. Roll two walnut-sized balls of skintone paste and press them firmly into the front and back parts of the male torso. Cut off any excess paste with a palette knife and make sure the edges are smooth. Remove both parts and join them together with gum arabic glue.

While the paste is soft, work quickly to define the facial features if the mould is not very precise. Indent the eye sockets with a small ball tool and use a fine modelling stick to emphasise the shape of the nose. Form a beard by scratching the chin with a scriber. Cut off the lower portion of the torso at the hips and bend the head forward slightly. Set aside the completed torso to dry.

Take another ball of skintone paste, this time about the size of a golf-ball: roll it into a sausage so that it is slightly longer than the man's torso, then flatten each end. Mould the feet at one end so that one foot appears to be turned slightly sideways. Indent some ridges into the paste to give the impression of legs and leave to dry. Then attach the legs to the torso with royal icing.

Make the arms by rolling two small sausages of paste and moulding them to shape. Attach these in position with a little royal icing and support them until dry with small blocks of polystyrene foam.

Use the same technique to mould the female figure but do not remove the lower part of the torso. Bend the figure forward into a sitting position. The lower limbs are shaped from a solid block of paste and left to dry, then they are attached to the torso with royal icing.

Paint the features on both figures using a no. 00 fine sable paintbrush and concentrated paste food colours. Highlight the cheeks, nose and forehead with very pale skintone dusting powder. Pipe Joseph's hair in chestnut royal icing using a no. 1.5 piping tube (tip), then brush it with a damp paintbrush and leave to dry. Highlight the hair and beard with flecks of chestnut and black.

MAKING THE CRIB

Cut the crib from dark brown paste, see page 73. Dry thoroughly before assembling with brown icing. Cut a rectangle of deep cream paste and fringe the edges with a craft knife. Position this in the crib. Then cut a rectangle of white paste for a blanket and drape it over .

PLEATING PASTILLAGE

Use cocktail sticks (toothpicks) to make pleats or folds in a thin piece of pastillage. Arrange the sticks side by side and lay the paste on top, then remove every other stick from underneath and lay on top of the paste, directly above its original position. Press down gently and the paste will form a concertina. Remove all the sticks and gather the ridges together.

Side Design

DRESSING THE FIGURES

To dress the figures, the paste must be rolled paper thin, see thickness guide on page 10, so it is most important that the pastillage is very elastic. Follow Pastillage recipe No. 3 on page 10.

Joseph

Roll out two small rectangles of paste slightly longer than the length of the arms and wrap one piece around each arm, gluing them into place with gum arabic glue. Pinch the upper edges into the shoulders and make pleats with a fine veining tool.

Roll out another piece of paste which is twice as wide as his torso and pleat it to fit the upper body, gluing it across the shoulders and under the neck. Make the gown out a rectangle of cream paste cut longer than the entire figure and about three times its width. Cut one corner off and fold the rest into pleats, then attach the paste at the shoulder and the waist. Drape the excess paste to the back of the figure.

Make the cloak from a rectangle of red-brown paste, cutting one end to form a semi-circle. Pleat the top and stick it to the back of the neck with gum arabic glue. Roll a collar so that one edge is thicker than the other and attach it to the cloak. Cut a belt from a fine strand of paste and snip the end to form the tassel.

Mary and Child

Roll out a rectangle of cream paste, the same length as the figure and four times its diameter. Moisten the neck line, the shoulders and the waist with gum arabic glue, then very carefully fold and pleat all the material to fit around the figure. Cut off any excess from the hem or back with scissors.

Make the baby from a narrow cone of paste and indent a slight bulge at the top for its head. Mark the features of the face with a ball tool, then wrap it up in a small pastillage blanket. Attach the baby to Mary's lap with a little royal icing.

Mould Mary's arms and hands. Cut the sleeves from squares of cream paste and frill one edge of each to form the cuffs. Pinch in at the shoulders and attach to the figure so that the arms appear to be holding the baby. Make Mary's cloak as for Joseph's; however, note that it should be slightly smaller and that it has no collar. Cut strands of hair from very thin pastillage using a sharp knife and stick them onto the head with gum arabic glue. Make the headscarf from a semi-circle of white paste and drape it around the head.

Side Designs

PAINTING ON ROYAL ICING

When you paint on royal icing, ensure that the icing is thoroughly dry before beginning. If there is any moisture in the icing, it will cause the food colour to run.

BYGONE DAYS

These children, with their wistful faces pressed against a shop window crammed with toys, evoke images of an earlier age.

20cm (8 inch) square cake
500g (1 lb) Marzipan (almond paste), see page 8
250g (8 oz/2 cups) Royal Icing, see page 9
red, jade, apple and moss green, dark brown, blue, pink, Cornish cream, lemon-yellow and black paste food colours
1.5kg (3 lb) Pastillage, see page 10
1.5kg (3 lb) Sugarpaste, see page 9
4 sheets leaf gelatine

EQUIPMENT

23cm (9 inch) square thin cake board
33 x 23cm (13 x 9 inch) rectangular cake board
nos. 0, 1 and 3 sable paintbrushes
set of modelling tools
no. 1 writing tube (tip) • piping bags
no. 381 straight frill cutter • scriber
cocktail sticks (toothpicks)
closed double scallop No. 13 mini crimper
confectioners' glaze
Gum Arabic Glue, see page 9
round garrett frill cutter • small carnation cutter
teardrop rose petal cutter

This cake is unusual in that, after it has been iced, it is stood on edge rather than on its base. Cut a wedge-shaped section from one edge, taking care to follow the angle indicated on the pattern, see page 51. The cake is coated in the laid-down position. Lay the cake on the 23cm (9 inch) thin cake board and cover it with marzipan and royal icing. Paint the top surface, which will be the shop window interior, and the brickwork of the outer walls, see diagram on pages 50 and 51. Use concentrated food colours diluted with a little water.

Cut out the shelves in pastillage, see page 50, and stick them to the window area. Cover the larger board with grey sugarpaste and use a straight edge or smoother to mark paving stones. Then stand the cake on end and fix it to the coated board with royal icing, positioning it about two-thirds away from one side of the board. Allow the cake to set in place before moving it.

Make a selection of small toys, see page 18, and attach them to the shelves, then put the cake to one side. You will need 500g (1 lb) of dark brown pastillage to make the panels for the bay window and door. Follow the patterns on page 50/51 to cut these pieces accurately as they must fit together closely when assembled.

Use royal icing to stick the window panels together and leave to set. Using a no. 1 piping tube (tip) pipe a line of red royal icing around the borders of the window. Add the decorative facia pieces and attach the pre-assembled window to the cake with a little royal icing.

Make the roof from two layers of pastillage. Colour 315g (10 oz) pastillage brick-red and roll it out very thin. Cut out the roof base and leave to dry for at least 24 hours. Make the strips of roof tiles and attach them to the base with gum arabic glue while they are still flexible. Leave to dry. Spread the angled roof of the cake with royal icing and fix the tiles in place. Support the corners until the roof has set firmly to the cake. Stick the door on the side of the cake. As a finishing touch, suspend a tiny holly wreath on the door, add the door step and hang the shop sign above the door.

MAKING THE WINDOW

The window consists of an outer pastillage frame which is assembled and dried before three inner panels are laid inside it. Leaf gelatine is attached to the inner panels with a minimum amount of royal icing otherwise the gelatine warps. The gelatine is sandwiched between the panels in the finished model. The pieces must be trimmed accurately and neatly to ensure they fit together.

1

2

1 To make the roof, cut about 36 strips and attach them to a pastillage base. Start at the bottom and work up to the top, overlapping the strips.
2 Pipe brown royal icing along the edges of the outer panels and stick them together; support on polystyrene to dry. Stick gelatine window panes to inner panels with icing; dry. Stick inner panels inside outer frame, sandwiching gelatine; leave to dry.

MAKING THE TILED ROOF

The tiled roof of the toyshop is made up from a series of strips of thin pastillage cut with a straight frill cutter. If you do not have the right cutter, cut plain strips and mark the edges of the tiles with a modelling tool.

HANDY HINT

Every keen cake decorator should reserve a piece of husk from the outside of a corn cob. When dried, attach the husk to a small piece of stiff card and keep it in your workbox. Use it whenever you want to impress a knitting-like texture into paste. A piece of raffia may be used instead.

MODELLING THE CHILDREN

To make the figures, mix the remaining white sugarpaste with the remaining pastillage. Prepare portions in the following colours: white, black, grey, golden yellow, lemon, skintone, olive green, light green, dark green, pink, red, blue and dark brown. Use the medium head impression on the mould for the larger children and the smallest impression for the two smaller characters. The heads must be made and thoroughly dried before assembling the figures. Pipe the hair on the large boy's head and use a paintbrush to style it. Leave to dry.

GIRL IN PINK HAT

Start with the legs by rolling two sausages of black paste. Turn 1cm (½ inch) over at each end to form the boots. Shape the wrinkles, heel and sole with the blade modelling tool and mark holes for bootlaces. Cut small rectangles of white paste for pantaloons and frill their edges. Then fold them around the legs. Stick the legs together and pin them onto a block of polystyrene so that they dry in position, with one leg extended slightly. When dry, cover with a red petticoat and a circular green skirt, which has been crimped and frilled as shown. Hang these on a pin to dry into shape, then stick them into position at the front of the shop window using royal icing.

Roll out some pale green paste and use a carnation cutter to make a frill for the waist band. Roll a short sausage for the bodice. Make the arms from two thin sausages of paste, with indentations at the ends. Make the hands, see page 17. Do not attach the arms or hands until the figures on each side of girl are in position.

Roll out some pale yellow paste and cut it into fine strands, then wrap these strands around cocktail sticks (toothpicks) to form ringlets of hair. Remove the sticks before the paste sets and glue the ringlets to the head with gum arabic glue. Make the brim of the hat using the rose petal cutter: frill it, then shape the crown from a flattened ball of paste and place it on the brim. Attach a ribbon bow to the back. Make the loops of the bow over the end of a cocktail stick.

BOY

Make the body by rolling a sausage of grey paste. Cut the lower third into two with a sharp knife, then mould the split ends to form the legs. Mark the trouser turn-ups with a modelling knife and make creases at the back of the knees. Pin the body onto a piece of polystyrene and adjust the legs to dry in the position illustrated in the close up photograph, see page 77.

To make the boots, bend two small pieces of black paste into an 'L' shape and mark the heels, wrinkles, and boot lace holes. Attach cocktail sticks (toothpicks) to the boot tops and leave to dry. Apply two coats of confectioners' glaze. Remove the sticks and attach the boots to the base of the trousers with royal icing.

Make the jumper by rolling out a rectangular piece of golden yellow paste. Use a piece of dried corn husk to imprint the knitting-like texture into it. Wrap the paste around the body with the seam line positioned at the front of the figure where it will not be seen. Make the arms out of yellow paste as well but do not insert the hands until after the figure is completed.

Set the body in position against the window, then attach the arms with royal icing. Make the hands, see page 17, and insert them into the sleeves, setting them in position on the window frame. The head with piped hair should now be attached with royal icing. Wrap a pastillage scarf around the neck to conceal the join. Lastly, attach a cap to the back of the head.

GIRL WITH PLAITS

Model a small sausage of white paste and divide the lower portion in two. Roll these ends to form two points. Make a short sausage of brown paste, cut it in half to make a pair of brown boots, both equal in size. Hollow the top of the boots and stick them to the ends of the legs with gum arabic glue. Suspend the body on a pin to dry as for the boy.

To dress the figure, pleat and frill a pink rectangle of paste and wrap it around the torso. The coat is made from a blue rectangle of paste which has one pleat at the back and lapels at the front. Make the arms and hands and stick them in position. Attach the head to the body and wrap a collar around the neck, then insert a red scarf under the collar.

The hair is added after the head is in place, so make sure that it is firmly attached. Roll a long thin strip of paste and use the edge of a fine palette knife to fringe it in long strands, leaving about 2.5cm (1 inch) uncut. Plait the cut strands, then glue the uncut section to one side of the head with gum arabic glue to give a centre parting. Make another plait in the same way and then glue it to the other side.

Place the child in front of the window such that the arm of the girl in the pink hat reaches out to hold one of the plaits.

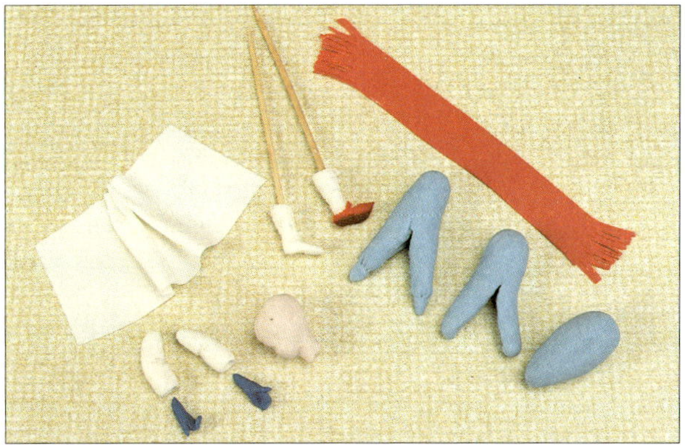

THE TODDLER

Make the socks on two cocktail sticks (toothpicks), as for feet, and turn up the toes. Leave to dry before wrapping a strip of red paste around the foot to form the shoes. Cut tiny figure-of-eight shapes for the soles.

The body is made from a short cone. The narrow end of the cone is split in two and shaped to fit into the top of the socks. Wrap a smock around the upper body with the opening down the back. Attach the head at the correct angle and leave it to dry, supported on polystyrene blocks. Add a large scarf. Attach the toddler to the shop front with royal icing and position the arms so that the hands are holding the window sill.

INDEX